Darfur

ROAD TO GENOCIDE

BAHAR ARABIE

authorHOUSE®

AuthorHouse™
1663 Liberty Drive
Bloomington, IN 47403
www.authorhouse.com
Phone: 1 (800) 839-8640

Published by AuthorHouse 06/14/2018

ISBN: 978-1-5462-4669-5 (sc)
ISBN: 978-1-5462-4667-1 (hc)
ISBN: 978-1-5462-4668-8 (e)

Library of Congress Control Number: 2018907034

Print information available on the last page.

Contents

CHAPTER ONE

ℬeginnings

The western Sudan region of Darfur was known in the past for its long history of statehood,mosaic ethnic groups, and rich and diverse culture. Long before the Sudan became a state, Darfur had for centuries its own identity and organized polity and system of governing. In 1873 by a twist of fate it became part of or rather appendex of Nile valey instead of the Sahel region or Chad basin where it naturally belongs and finds itself at ease. Unlike other regions of Sudan,Darfur was incorporated in to Sudan by use of brute force. First in 1872 when the Sultanate was invaded and conqured by the slave merchant Zebier Rahma Mansor on behalf of Turko Egyptian administration in the Nile valley,but reverted back to independence in 1899, and again in 1916 when invaded by the Anglo Egyptian colonial administration in Khartoum and annexted to Sudan.

With the turn of the twenty first centuray the name Darfur, up to the writing of this memoir became synonymous with disaster, tragedy, crisis, atrocity, suffering, and survival. Since 2003, Darfur has been under siege by its own Sudanese national government and its allied militias, known by various names as time goes on,(Janjaweed,The fearful and light and fast, the rapid support force etc) with no sign of cessation of hostilities in sight but imposition of calm by brute force, no alleviation of the suffering. Hundreds of thousands dead; millions displaced and on the brink of death. Tragedy and fear, despair and uncertainty became the order of the day and the new normal. While governments and the international community argue about Darfur and the human rights violations committed there, the humans continue to face violation, starvation, death, genocide by attrition, and complete change of their way of life.

How Darfur the once beautiful, peaceful, and serene land came to this is my story. It is the story of every Darfuri from Kefiakangi to Owenat, from Tine to Sharif-kabashi, a story of various tribes of Benga, Kerisha and Bagara of the south, and Zaghawa, Massalit, Fur, Tunjur and Midop of the west and north, as well as a story of Berti, Bergid and others in the east. Whether I am a good teller of the story, or good narrator of the historical oral tradition corroborated by documented events I will leave to the judgment of the reader. This story is also my perspective a recount of my own story and observations and participation in these events, a recounting of my contribution to the struggle of the people of Darfur towards self-realization and freedom. I write so that truth as I expreiced it will be known to succeeding generations

Before I became the teller of this tale, I was Bahradin. Like many Zaghawa families and households who cherish and commemorate the nobles and notables of the land, I was probably named by my father after the Sultan Bahradin of Dar Massalit, or Amir Bahradin, son of Sultan Ali Dinar. Often times he fondly called me Amir!but not Sultan, obviously because I was his favorite. To the rest of the family, I was simply Bardin. My mother favored to call me *Derea* - the shield – and also *Amir* - the prince - of the family.

I am the son of Hoqi Eram, Arabicised to Faki Ibrahim, a prominent religious healer in the cluster of villages in the small locality of Oro of Dar Toweir. He was the son of Arbi, the son of Hesien, the son of Adam Morme, the son of Tejero, the son of Hoqi, the son of Midoye, great-grandson of Karta the son of Nedy, great-grandson of Deqin the son of Omat - better known as Mahamat Bornawe, the son of Haj Ali.

My mother, Gania (changed to Khatra in Arabic documents), a woman in the environtment of traditionally conservative Zaghaqa society was of strong will, rare courage, and independent Opinion, She was the only child of her mother Hawa Hari, and the daughter of Haron, the son of Njorom, the son of Arko, the son of Bodi, the son of Adalla, who was also great-grandson of Karta from whom my father's family descended. In Zaghawa tradition they were distant cousins.

My grand mother Hawa Hari was the sister of the legendry Esakha

Hari, better known as Esakha Tamara the Red-Headed, the venerated and charismatic Eladegain leader. When I was a child, my grandmother and the other village elders told stories about Tamara and the many battles he fought to defend the fatherland from marauding Arabs who sought to seize the land and enslave its people and in the service of Sultanate of Darfur's army.

My name, both Arabic and Islamic in origin and meaning, reflected my father's deep respect for the Darfur Sultans and their descendants. When I enrolled at the primary school, it was further Arabicised in the quest by Khartoum authorities to Arabize every non-Arab group and person. In the Sudano Lavantine tradition of standard Arabic, I was called Bahreldin Ibrahim Arabie, known in later years as Bahar Arabie.

Due to the absence of birth records, I do not know exact date of my birth,but only sure of my birth place, which is the ancestral village of Yakesie in Oro. My birth date could be some time between 1954 and 1957. I adopted 1957 as the year of my birth and chose January 1st as my birthday, as do most of the Sudanese without a birth certificate, because January 1st is the day of Sudan's declaration of independence.

My mother had two girls before me: Zerga the eldest, and Sonda, who later went by the Arabicized name of Aisha at school. After me, Mother had six other children: Eshaq, Nora, Deli, Aziza, Hawa, and Farah. Deli, Aziza, and Hawa died before the age of five from the measles, whooping cough, and lack of adequate medical care. Nora, whom I dearly loved, died tragically, but that dark event comes later in my story. Zerga, my mother's first, was the pillar of the household until she was given away in marriage. She was a rare human being of light spirit and an easy going sense of humor. She died in a tragic motor accident at age 57 and was survived by many children.

My father had two children from earlier marriage, with aunt Khadoj, whom I never met as she died many years before even my father married my mother, my elder two half siblings are Halom and Abdelkarim better known as Ediah. As I grew up I come to know both of them as my full siblings, as we all lived in the same household, and my mother who is their step mother became like their real mother. After my mother, my father also married aunt Zainaba and had five children with her, Khatra, Gesaima, Hasania, Heriya and Amir

My father combined religious healing with other means of Zaghawa livelihood. He was also a herder and farmer, and at times the village Imam and trader in sugar, tea, and palm dates. I was his favorite companion and accompanied him on many of his various travels, whether to markets out side Dar Zaghawa to sell rams and camels and purchase millet for the family in bad years, or on his healing contracts to various parts of Dar Zaghawa, or to buy sugar and tea leaves from another trader in a far away village.

Politically, he was an Ansar, a supporter of Almahdi's family and the Umma party. Almahdi, also known as Mohammed Ahmed Abdalla, who led a religious war from the village of Jazira Aba on the White Nile against the Turco-Egyptian authorities in the Nilotic Sudan in 1885. He defeated the feebled Turkish authority in Sudan and established the Mahdist state, which was overthrown by the British in 1998. After Sudan gained independence from the British in 1956, Almahdi's son, Abdulrahaman Almadi, established the Umma Party, which is until today a major poltical force.

My father spent many years of his youth at Jazira Abba, where he was initiated to Ansar's *Sufi* sect and committed Almahdi's *Ratib* –book of prayers-to memory before returning to Dar Zaghawa in the early forties. In his presence he will not allow anybody to speak ill of Almahdi's family or the Umma party.

After Sudan gained independence in 1956 and party politics came in to full play throughout Sudan, my father was one of the few literate Umma members who helped establish the party structures in northern Darfur. He vied with Mahmoud Altyb, a cousin of the Shertai Tijani Altyb of Dar Gala, for the party nomination to contest the election to represent the north western Darfur district, the 149 constituency at the national parliament. Mahmoud Altyb won the nomination and became the candidate and eventually the election, and went to Khartoum to represent the district on the national stage. My father did not venture in to politics again.

Our family is from the Ela-deqin or Ela-degain clan of the greater Zaghawa tribal group, traditionally from Northern Darfur and North eastern Chad, but presently spread to all corners of Darfur. My clan is called Ela-degain because tradition has it that we are descendants of Deqin, the son of Mahamat Bornawe, the son of Haj Ali.

Mahamat Bornawe, from whom my forefathers descended, was a Muslim and a son of a Muslim. He was either an immigrant or a refugee in what is known today as Beri Beih or Dar Zaghawa, from the region of Bornu in Northern Nigeria and North western Chad.

The exact date of Mohamat Bornawe's arrival and settlement in this region, and the circumstances behind his displacement and settlement in this area, are not precisely known due to lack of historical records. Depending on the memory of elders as handed down to them by their elders as far back as thirteen or fourteen generations, Mahamat Bornawe's arrival to the area must have been in the late fifteenth century.

The oral tradition of the elders also tells us better about the exact location of his home, water supply source, as well as his three sons and two daughters, who were Dore, Deqin, Kadawo, Noqui and Agab.

According to ela-Degain oral account, his home was said to been the top of mount Ebi-ere' in the Joktara area of Dar Toweir. His water source was said to be the well of *Bir Bameshi*. It could be that this land looked differently in those days than today's sand strewen waste. Whether Mohamat Bornawe came alone or with a group in which he was a leader, the tradition tells us very little and instead attempts to circumvent these facts, as with most of Islamized Sudanic groups who find some sense of Islamic originality by magnifying and adopting certain wise Arab folk heroes, which were said to have migrated from South Arabia to North Africa, and then marauded to the Sahel region.

Eventually some or one of them voluntarily or otherwise intermarried with Bornawe's ancestors and produced an offspring. The tradition also tells us at the time Mahamat Bornawe had his campfire on top of Mount Ebi-ere, the surrounding country was almost unpopulated but rich with vegetation. The tradition goes that there were few other camp fires which could be seen from great distances, as the nights in those days were said to be much darker than presently. One of those was said to be a fire on Mount Darma, west of the present town of Foraweya.

The relics associated with Mahamat Bornawe tell us that he was with a community and was able in tandem to dig wells, defend and provide security for themselves, and delimit the area of their habitat and domain.

There was no government in their life yet they were not savage but, highly organized, but with no terrorizing greedy tax collectors and gun- totting or baton-wielding police whose sight sends shivers in the spines of the law-abiding and peace-loving before those with issues in their bags. The only authority in their life was the authority of the elders and the traditional leadership, which was attached to the Sultanate by nominal and subtle rules and norms, which was viewed as almost divine and obeyed, like answering the body's need for food and water.

Mahamat Bornawe and his people were nomads and subsistent farmers and hunters of giraffe and deer, which were said, abound in the marshes and forest fringed seasonal lakes of Wadis Hawar in the north and Seyra in the south. Hunting on horseback with long spears was said to be the pride of these people. They were also great builders, bearers of traditional civilized building, as the top of Ebi-ere stands witness today to their huge rock dwellings.

Historically the region from which Mohamed Bornawe came from was under the empire of Kanem, established by Zaghawa in the early eleventh century. The Kanem empire and its tributary states extended at its peak from the border with the seven Hausa kingdoms of Northern Nigeria in the west, to the regions immediately west of the Nile River in the east, and from Southern Libya or Fezan in the north, to the rain forests of Cameroon and Central African Republic in the south. It began declining in power and authority around the middle of the fifteenth century due to internal weaknesses and persistent attacks from outside enemies, especially by slave raiders from the greater Maghreb region, and from hostile and destructive Bulala tribal groups within the empire itself. That period witnessed both great social and political upheavals.

The story of the decline of Kanem Empire bears similarities with decline of the Funj power and ascendancy of the Hamaj in the Nilotic Sudan, which was also accelerated by in fightings and internecine wars among its princes and nobility who sought to escape the many crises of their empire by indulging in feuds and apportioning blames, and between the regional commanders of its armies and subordinate rulers, resulting in opportunistic foreign enemies taking advantage of and descending on its territories and domains.

The political institutions of the empire, as told by the few European and Arab travelers of the time, were very similar to the institutions of Songhai and Mali in the West and of the Kira and the Funj kingdoms which came into being in later centuries in Sudan.

History tells us that Kanem as empire collapsed and Njemi its capital, which was said to be on the shores of Lake Chad, was destroyed. Whoever survived from the hires to the power and a larger section of its nobility moved westward to salvage whatever remained of their empire in the region known today as Bornu. Their capital was established at a place known as Anzergamo, a well-known site in the present day Borno State of Nigeria.

From Anzergamo, the surviving rulers extended their authority farther east and west and adopted the name Kanem Bornu to their new domains. The collapse of Kanem and the disintegration of its social, economic, and political structure led some commanders, regional rulers, lords, and magnets to seek refuge else where, with their followers mostly out of the domain of Kanem.

One historical hypothesis which can be deduced is that in the absence of archeological evidence, Amara Dongus, founder of the Funj kingdom and his warrior group the Funj, could be a product of those Kanem commanders, because the events which led to the formation of the statehood - which still bewilders students of Sudanese history - reflect the character and pedigree of those who made it possible, plus the names Amara, Donqas, Deqin, and Funj (or Funi) are abound today from Dar Zaghawa to the Bornu region.

It is also a tradition of Zaghawa for whole clans to migrate long distances away from their homeland in years of drought and famine. One such migration probably occurred in the early eighteenth century, on a difficult year, when a section of the ela-Dore clan with the king of Dar Toweir settled in Kajmar in Kurdofan. As time passed the migrants to Kurdofan were completely absorbed in the Arabized culture of their neighbors, but still identified themselves as Zaghawa. In more recent times, when the Zaghawa were displaced by drought in North Darfur in the late sixties and early seventies, they migrated with the king of Dar Toweir, Malik Ali Mohammadian, to South Darfur. While Malik eventually returned to his domain in Omborow due to governmental pressure, a sizable number of the Zaghawa from Toweir and other Zaghawa dars remained in South Darfur.

As a child, I used to listen to an old folk song, said to be sang by a blacksmith maid during the Deqin era. It goes like this:

Mai yo, Beri Yo, Deqin Bagowe
Bado yo omo yo, Deqin Bagowe.

No blacksmith, no Beri left [in the father land],
it is the era of Deqin
No antelope no ostrich left [in the father land],
it is the era of Deqin

One of the descendants of Bornawe named Amara was also said to have left the king's town on Mount Ebi-ere with followers after a quarrel with the king, and built stone dwellings resembling a fortress in Shereyo village in Joktara. They later left the country with many other Zaghawas when draught and famine became so devastating, but the exact date of this event is unknown. Likewise, the founders of the Dajo kingdom and the Tunjur, who still retain kinsfolk in Chad, which was subsequently succeeded by the Fur, could be along this line of Kanem's displaced rulers in the wilderness.

Kanem's fall and the resultant socio-political chaos must have led to a great humanitarian crisis,in terms of that era which could have been for them, even larger in magnitude and worse in severity than the one in Darfur today, given the size of the area and populations involved. How long that crisis lasted is a matter of conjecture. It could have been decades or it could have lasted several hundred years, judging by the extremely difficult times of that period.

The original Zaghawa who founded Kanem must have dispersed and scattered; many of their tribes lost their identity and became non-Beri speaking people, or simply absorbed into other larger groups. It is evident from history that although Zaghawas were great warriors with established states, they were culturally weak and adopted the customs of other conquered groups, which might explain how they lost their language. Likewise, other people must have been assimilated within the Zaghawa and became *Beri*, a term used by Zaghawa to refer to their tribe and themselves.

One fact which can be deduced is that, the crisis which befell Kanem must have generated other crises, and each crisis in turn triggered more crises, ranging from wars by invaders or between tribal groups, for land or property, to hunger, or starvation, and famine. Whole groups must have disappeared or perished when they were forced to leave their traditional homes. In the process, huge numbers of displaced persons banded together for protection and sustenance, gradually became tribal enclaves, or *Dars*. The sociological inevitability of living together for long periods of time caused them to integrate and assimilate through marriage, affinity, and communal sharing of natural resources. The people became one community, speaking one language or dialect and adopting the same customs and traditions, thus creating a new culture and ethnic group.

This progression continued through the centuries in the Sahel region. Groups formed alliances to protect themselves from the slave traders raids and from other hostile groups, or fled the area altogether. Whole groups also fragmented because of fights over land or other property. What were two groups one day might become one group the next day; or one group might split into two groups.

This in part explains the many similarities and common cultures between the peoples of the Sudanic belt, from Senegal to Kurdofan. One can hardly tell the difference in appearance, culture, and way of life between a Walof in Senegal and Mali and a Zabarma in Niger, or a Hausa or Kanuri in Northern Nigeria and a Bagirma or Belala in Chad, or between a Zaghawa, Tunjur, Fur, and Berti in Chad and Sudan. They share a common ancestry, a common ethos, uprooted and displaced once upon a time by great and terrible calamities, whether wars or environmental conditions or slave trader raids.

In this process of displacement, the original Zaghawas were constantly on the move throughout the centuries to the east and west of their original home. Those who were able to maintain the original culture and language moved from their larger traditional home of Northwestern Chad and Southern Libya eastward, to adopt their present Dar, extending from the Southern Tibesti Mountains to the north east of Jebel Marra, as did the Tunjur, Berti, Dajo, Fur, Massalit and other Darfur and Kurdofani groups who share a common ancestry with old Zaghawa. Other groups came from the east, especially from the Nile basin, and integrated with these Saharan Sudanic groups.

Mahamat Bornawe was a creature of his era and its difficult circumstances. He could be part of those groups who were dispersed after the collapse of Kanim. He must have come with his group to Dar Toweir from the Lake Chad region or Yerwa in present day Maiduguri after a long and arduous journey. Driven by security and necessity, others of his kinsfolk also came to Dar Gala, Dar Kobe, and Dar Artaj.

It is difficult to find a convenient justification for his settlement in this area other than that the area was climatically similar to where he came from. More specifically, he was a nomadic pastoralist. It is easier to adduce why he adopted the nick name Bornawe, which has no ethnic significance,but encapsulates the isentity and belonging to a locality in the region.

It is yet to be a verified fact that all present Zaghawas came to their present land from West or Northwest Chad with their way of life, which was herding. How many of them or who came from Kanem or Borno and at what periods of time, whether before or after Mahamat Bornawe, is a matter for speculation. The present day Borno region is a mosaic of ethnic groups and tribes which speak different languages, but none calls itself Zaghawa or Beri or speak their language, aside from the Kanuri, the tribe of the rulers of Bornu, which call themselves Beri-Beri and some how bear similar facial features with the Zaghawa. The Borno people, especially the traditional ruling class of the Kanuri, are aware of the historical roots and role played by the ancient Zaghawa in the establishment of the Kanem Empire.

Who else were the natives of the present locality of Dar Zaghawa is a matter of speculation. Some argue, without concrete evidence that before the Zaghawa moved in, the area was long inhabited by a small group called *Mai* in Zaghawa and *Hadahid* in Arabic. The Mai, once stigmatized and virtually segregated from the Zaghawa, are indispensable to the Zaghawa life. When and why were they called Mai and relegated to their servile and demeaned position, no clear explanation can be given. Ironically, the word Mai meant "supreme ruler" during the Kanem Empire, while in West Africa it means today the overlord or master or owner of a property. Could it be that the Mais of Dar Zaghawa were the indigenous people, submerged by overwhelming waves of Zaghawa immigrants, or are they descended from the banished Mais from Kanem, or are they actual ancient Mais of the territory? It is hard to say; however their segregation is fast disappearing in the cities and towns of Sudan, though discrimination in marriages still persists.

Growing up in Dar Zaghawa

As mentioned before, this is my story within the wider Zaghawa and Darfur story. It is a recount of personal experiences and perspective at various stages of my involvement in the story of the people and my role and contribution to the struggle of the people of Darfur towards self realization and freedom. I wrote it so that truth will be known to generations yet to be born, for them to pass judgment on what we did.

In this I do not claim that I have told every thing to be told or gave the personalities mentioned in this writing their due right, but at least I have given them every respect they deserve. I also knew I have left out many people in my story for the sake of making a long story short. This by no means intended to ignore their roles. In telling my story I will not follow the pattern whereby people begin the writing of their experiences with details on their birth, upbringing, and careers, up to the time they were writing.

In this work I will differ. Suffice it that I gave a brief introductory account to the story of Zaghawa, instead I will deviate from that tradition, simply because it is not much different than any other life story of an average, educated Darfuri.

I was born in a typical, traditional family household. As a child, I became a baby sitter to my younger sister Nora for two seasons, until she learned to walk. I loved Nora the way a parent loves a child. I carried her on my back while our mother worked in the field, or gathered wild cereals and fruits, or watered the herds and filled water skins. When Nora cried, I sang her lullabies until she fell asleep. Then I was free to play in the sand with Eshaq or join Mother at work, when she would tell me an old folk story or a joke.

At age six I became a junior herder, then eventually a senior herder to my family's herd of goats, sheep, and camels. I gathered fire wood and drew water from the well to fill troughs for the herds and water skins for the family. Later I attended boarding school. I endured the physical and psychological hardships experienced by almost all in the Zaghawa country side, where water was and is still scarce,food a precious commodity, and domestic animals a treasure, because they are the bedrock of our livelihood and of the economy.

I progressed through schools,and as time went by moved from Dar Zaghawa country side to towns as my education demanded. My view for the world and the Sudan also changed with education and maturity in age.

And so life progressed, with nothing out of the ordinary occurring until 1977, when the Darfuris, for the first time, spoke loudly in unity and with one voice. Before going in to that I think it is in order to set the scene

CHAPTER TWO

Ombadda in the late 70s and early 80s

The western Omdurman suburb of Ombadda was a relatively small suburban town in the mid-seventies, mostly inhabited by people of Northern or riverine extraction. Its urban development was slow and minimal and followed the same pattern of the old town. The population came from the old town in that they were mostly riverine, sophisticated, and well-connected to the elite and the privileged in old Omdurman and Khartoum.

In the mid-seventies, a new phenomenon developed. People of mostly Western Sudan origin – a mosaic of African and Arab descents - left their rented homes in the three cities of Khartoum, Omdurman, and Khartoum North and began building, without regard to town planning rules and regulations, very crude structures of mud and dung at the outskirts of the triangular capital, particularly to the west of Ombadda. Much to the chagrin of privileged Khartoumers and Omdurmanese, a new market also appeared between Old Omdurman and Ombadda. The traders were mostly Westerners and on display in this market were high quality goods imported from Libya. In contrast to goods in the main markets, the Libyan goods were superior and affordable.

To the growing dismay of the Omdurmanese, these Westerners did not go away. They grew in numbers as other family members also joined them and their businesses prospered. These Westerners were trying to make a living for themselves after drought destroyed their farms and pastures, which led to the loss of their herds - the backbone of their livelihood.

Others faced quarrels with family members over property and dwindling fortunes and were forced to pursue a different career, usually in trading, to support their families. For others, Ombadda was a stopover as they sought to migrate to Libya or Saudi Arabia in search of a better life. Whatever the reason, each came to Khartoum with high hopes and expectations of success.

Faced with the reality that the "Gharaba," or those from the West, weren't leaving, the Omdurmanese turned to the municipal and provincial authorities to push them out. The government viewed Westerners with a suspicious eye, and perceived the newly set up structures as possible sanctuaries for its opponents, called the Mercenaries, who once attempted and nearly succeeded to topple the regime of Ja'afar Nemairy, with the help of the Libyan-based National Front.

The authorities moved in with bulldozers and manual demolishers. Within a short period, thousands of so-called unplanned structures were leveled to the ground. But as quickly as the authorities demolished by day, the Westerners just as quickly erected new structures by night on the same spots. It was like a game of cat and mouse, though the determination of the Westerners surpassed that of the authorities'. The displaced were united in purpose,even though lacked in resources but did not lack the ingenuity and organization to restore their huts back to where they believed they belonged, like the rest of the old city dwellers.

Their organizations and associations petitioned the government as true and bona fide citizens of the country who had every right to live wherever they wanted to live. They demanded the right to be allowed to build their houses in their nation's capital without harassment.

As their determination grew, the authorities ran out of room to maneuver and began to back-pedal, instead they began speaking of surveying the area and planning buildings. The demolition had been undertaken at a great cost, which the Khartoumers and Omdurmanese were unable or unwilling to reimburse, while the Libya traders of the West were willing to placate the authorities and pay their taxes and dues and were in no hurry to demand services from the government.

The authorities relented for some time before dividing the area in to sections, giving each section an identification number and a committee to follow up on its development. This led to the Khartoumers stereotyping and stigmatizing the area and its people. They attached labels such as the Ghetto area and Slum area, or collectively, *Ombadda Almesih* – the slums.

The inhabitants, however, named their town *Omdurman Algadida* or New Omdurman, and its suburbs mostly reflected the localities or regions from where they came.

Throughout the narrow alleyways of the walled huts and hutches of Ombadda Almesih, the poverty and misery of the people were evident. Nevertheless, the women gave the impression that though poor, they lacked neither the dignity nor generosity of the West. They tried their best to copy the culture of the Khartoum lady or the Jalaba woman in dress and scent. Even in food and domestic household arrangements, the Northern life style overshadowed the traditional Darfuri or Kurdufani life style. The men, too, copied the characteristics of the riverine men of the North both in dress and speech.

Though the Almesih community was excluded from Khartoum scheme of things, it believed the Sudan was its ultimate country and home and were ready to embrace the Khartoum way of life.

If the government was worried about their presence in the outskirts of the capital and their unemployment, they need not have. The people of Almesih would not bother the government with the problems of unemployment. Instead, they would create their own jobs or migrate abroad, and send remittances to help both their families and the government.

It was in such circumstances that I arrived in the capital in the autumn of 1977 with the hope of continuing my studies at the university or obtain a copy of my Sudan General Education Certificate, which in those days enabled one to get a popular teaching job with the Ministry of Education. I also sought to apply for study abroad on scholarship, in case I was not admitted in to the elite Khartoum University, more especially at the time Egypt provided thousands of scholarship opportunities for Sudanese students. I realized that scholarships especially the Egyptian scholarships are exclusive for privileged revirain students or Nemairy's Mayoist regime loyalists from other parts of the Sudan.

I lodged with relatives who were struggling to survive in Ombadda *Almesih* as I waited for the results of admission tests. With the help of the Late Dr Sid Ahmad Nugdalla I ended up enrolling in the School of Extra-Mural Studies of the University of Khartoum, now known as Faculty of technological and developmental studies and for the next three years was a part of the university academia and Khartoum life. Those three years were formative,and accorded me the opportunity to realize the extend of privilege the riverine Sudanese enjoyed in terms of social,political and economic resources of the country, to the exclusive detriment of all other Sudanese. This was most apparent in the University in both students and faculty. In my class of thirty seven I was the only one from Darfur,one from the South,and two from South Kurdofan,the rest are riverine northern Sudanese. I studied social work and sociology, which opened for me new horizons of thinking to the Sudanese phenomenon and the real Sudanese situation. I also realized to what extend the Jallabas or people of the Northern orgin looked down at other Sudanese, and exercised a subtle discrimination against them in all walks of life. For them the Sudan is their own. Other groups are either third or second class citizens,good only to be servants for the first class. I experienced this in personal terms,perhaps it is appropriate to mention this here as an example.

At the beginning of my studies I tried to make friends with some of my class mates from the northern region of the country. I had little success except with one of them,who showed great deal of interest in Darfur and people from Darfur "Nas Darfur" as he called them. We used to discuss a lot about Khartoum life,music and musicians and foot ball or soccer. We even shared segarets or snuff and some times had bearkfast together. He encouraged me to visit his home in Omdorman and I did. I began to relate to him and the northerners in general. We rarely talked of politics any time I bring up the subject he would change it to sports or music. Then one day he shocked me,he said "I think you are too ambitious. If you continue like this one day you will become great like Abel Alier"! Abel Alier was the second vice president at the time,a black African from Dinka tribe of South Sudan. I said why not like Nemiery himself (Nemiery was the president at the time)here his demeanor changed and countered "that is impossible it seems you don't know your place in this society. I am telling you what you could possibly achieve for yourself" then he moved away with a stone face. Our friendship ended that day. He soon spread my statement to other class mates from the north,and I felt some degree of hostility from many of them. Some times I was mocked and pestered upon for the rest of our days at the school.

CHAPTER THREE

$\mathscr{F}$rom Sudan to Nigeria

After three years of hard work, and very difficult social and financial situation, I graduated with a diploma in Social Work. Like many new Darfuri graduates whose family and personal living conditions could be described as difficult at best, or mere survival at worst, a diploma meant a lot. It was a ticket to a job and a steady, if meager income, if there is a level playing field and all things are equal

I was both very young and ambitious in terms of what I could or wanted to achieve financially once I left Sudan. I thought about leaving the country, immigrating either to Europe or the USA, or even to Nigeria. The rich oil countries in the Persian Gulf and Libya were not particularly attractive to me simply because I had my own ideological and cultural bias which did not favor going to these Arab countries.

Nigeria was my favorite choice, because it has also emerged at the time as a major oil producing and exporting country with huge developmental needs in almost all fields. Northern Nigeria was also culturally similar to Sudan and had shared the same British Colonial experience.

The Sudanese and Sudan as a country had a lot of respect among Northern Nigerians at the time on account of being Islamic, and it lay on their pilgrimage route to Mecca. Many of their kin had settled in Sudan. Democratic Northern Nigeria looked to Sudan for assistance in its developmental efforts, especially in education. Sudanese were instrumental in establishing the Universities of Bayero at Kano and Ahmado Bello at

Zaria, as well as the judicial system when the North copied the Sudan legal system when it became independent.

Nigeria was also particularly attractive because some friends had already gone there and were doing well. Many of them were either teaching at schools or studying for degrees at the universities. One of these was Adam Shugar, a distant cousin. After graduation from Omdurman Islamic University, Shugar had a brief legal career before migrating to Nigeria years before. He had both a good teaching job and status in the main northern city, Kano.

I felt Nigeria offered the opportunity I yearned for, since it had more and better equipped universities than my country. I presented my plans to go to Nigeria to my small circle of relatives and friends, who, though skeptical about its expectations and promises of economic gain, agreed it was the best place to further my education.

One person who greatly encouraged me in my plans was my teacher and intellectual mentor, Dr. Sid Ahmad Nugdalla, Khartoum University professor and the Dean of the School of Extra-Mural Studies. A riverine Northerner who himself had been a struggler for self-education in his youth, Dr. Nugdalla and others of his school of thought helped shaped the intellectual identity and perception of many Northern Sudanese youths of that generation.

In a social environment held hostage by Nemairy policies of repression, suppression, and outright exclusion and marginalization, and despite harassment and intimidation from the regime's security agents, Nugdalla initiated the Arkaweet Conference. This forum held regular annual conferences which brought together intellectuals, academics, business entrepreneurs, government functionaries and other public spirited individuals from all walks of life to discuss the developmental needs of Sudan. Nugdalla also formed, in early 80s, a small forum known as the Thinkers' Forum, which regularly held debates and discussions on national issues in his office at the university every Tuesday night. He also inspired the like-minded through his writings in his weekly column in the daily newspaper, *Al-Ayam*.

This scholar and thinker devoted his intellectual work for the Sudan as he saw it: a cultural mosaic, with Arab culture defining its political identity. However, like the rest of the Northern elites and intellectuals, he wanted to see it continue as Arab country,dominated by the north and northern elite, despite his own Nubian and very African features and the country's African majority which was brutally marginalized.

As I raised funds for the cost of the trip, my network of relatives and friends proved to be indispensable. Ahmed Nehar, a cousin with a big heart and tremendous generosity, helped me with the greater part of the cost of the plane ticket to Kano, along with some pocket money. Other friends helped with advice about how to obtain the Nigerian entry visa, while others helped with connections with security operatives to secure the exit visa from the Ministry of Interior, which was very difficult in those days and needed a middle man to connect you to the passport officer. You also needed money for bribing an agent who had good connections with security officials, whom in those days of Nemairy's regime, held and controlled the country like a herd in a cattle pen.

Finally having all I needed, I made my reservations to depart Khartoum. A neighbor drove me to the airport in his old *Moscovich* taxi cab. As I got in the cab, I thought about my situation and my family in far away Darfur: father, mother, brothers and sisters, people to whom I was emotionally attached. I didn't know how they would receive the news of my departure from the country, as I did not write them earlier, which was the only means of communication in those days.

As I gazed out of the car window as we sped by the mud and wood huts of Ombadah-Fariek Alfashir, a poor suburb of new Omdurman, I was overwhelmed by the poverty, wretchedness, and helplessness of the place. The economic gap between the slum dwellers – people from Darfur, Kordofan, and South Sudan - and the original Khartoumers and Omdurmanians, the *Awlad Al Balad* - dwellers of Al Mulazmeen, Almorada, Alriyadh, Khartoum Amarat, and Al Safia - was so intimidating, so cruel, like an uncrossable abyss.

We approached the city, passing through dark alleyways. The only lights were feeble paraffin wax lamp lights in the hut windows; the only sounds heard were the cries of starving infants and children. We passed Toyota pickup trucks which were modified and fitted with seating to carry commuters on the streets, known as *Berinssa*. Their conductors called for passengers: *Ambada! Bir al-Omda, al- Arda, Mahata al-Wosta* – these were the stops along the small commuter bus routes.

As we moved through the dusty darkness toward the brightness of Omdurman city center, the streets became broader and paved, bordered by electric and telephone poles. The house compounds became bigger. They were red brick but painted white, gray or brown, with concrete and Zink roofs and electric lights brightening their interiors. It was an unforgetable contrast between poverty and well to do communities.

The neighbor cab driver spoke of the difficulties he and other taxi drivers face in trying to make ends meet, especially in getting the fuel *benzene* for their vehicles. Long hours were spent in endless queues at the fuel stations, the cost of the fuel on the black market ever rising, as did transport fares and food prices.

We agreed that the regime and its riverine Jallaba elites feared that a revolution by the hungry masses would break out in the heart of Khartoum, hence their outrageous attempts to herd them away from the capital under the pretext that they were illegal aliens from Chad or Ethiopia, or unwanted people which constituted a nuisance and security risk for Khartoum and its privileged people.

Even more worrisome for them was the teeming crowds were from the marginalized areas of Sudan, especially from Darfur, Nuba Mountain and the South. If revolution broke out and was successful, it would be the end of the Jallaba State and their monopoly of power, wealth and domination of the socio-cultural affairs of the country. That was a situation they would do everything possible to prevent from happening, and to prevent it they must expel and stop the unwanted mobs coming in droves in search of food, work and education.

We agreed that our people back home in Darfur suffered an even more bleak situation due to the neglect of the elite-centered and Northern-focused government. Their suffering was just as unquantifiable because it was so pervasive, starting with how to get drinking water, food, medicine, security, and education, as well as transportation, jobs, and how to improve the general welfare.

We also reflected on the Nemairy's newly decreed 1980 regional government law, which redivided the country into five regions - North, South, West, East, and Center – and merged Darfur with Kordofan, with al-Obaid as its capital.

The decision outraged and infuriated all Darfuris, and was seen as an insult and an affront by Darfur parliamentarians in the national assembly. The Parliamentarians protested inside the assembly while Nemairy was reading his speech on the division. In a show of megnanimity Nemairy immediately declared Darfur a separate region. A few days later he appointed a non-Darfuri governor to Darfur, while all other regions had their own sons as governors. This decision which was another manifestation of northern elite's disregard to the feelings of Darfuris,was an other affront to Darfuris, sending them a message that they were not trust worthy, incompetent and incapable of governing even their own region, which led to even more violent protests in Darfur itself. People demonstrated and clashed with security agents, with many of them killed or wounded. In Khartoum Darfuris held rallies and symposiums to discuss this insult. Those symposiums were vigilantly watched by Nemairy's secret service and security operatives. I could remember that at one of these symposiums a man of northern extraction, just snached the microphone and said "the government is here to protect every one, and if any one break the law the government will deal with him decisively. The government gave you this opportunity to express yourself, do not abuse it or else!". There was an implied threat in the statement,but no one cared at the time.

Fearing an outbreak of a civil war in Darfur, especially since the region was close to Libya, with whose Colonel Gaddafi he was at odds, Nemairy Who was not as blood thrusty as Albashir,quickly abrogated his presidential decree and appointed an ethnic Darfuri, Ahmad Diraige, as governor for the region.

Nemairy's decisions concerning Darfur and the events which followed were the defining moment for the Darfuri identity and character. For the first time in contemporary independent Sudan history, the people of Darfur banded together with a sense of oneness. They were united by a common purpose: the recognition of their identity and dignity by the Khartoum rulers. For the first time, Darfuris came out boldly and demanded their own separate region.

Meanwhile, the new Darfur governor, given his credentials and political experience as a former parliamentary opposition leader and his role in forming the Darfur Development Front, was best suited for the job. We hoped he would work toward the reawakening of Darfur and unite its people towards the common goals of socio-economic development and its cultural renaissance.

Our vehicle reeled into the city center, through al-Ardha and Hai al-Arab suburbs. At the city center, better known as *Mahata al-Wosta,* we managed to pass through a traffic jam and crowds of commuters struggling hand and foot to board the mini buses, the *Berinssat,* to different parts of the metropolis.

We passed the city center with its sounds, local music, and smells of restaurants to al-Moradda Street to get to the White Nile bridge - an old steel bridge constructed on the White Nile River by the British during the Colonial Era - to connect Khartoum on the other side of the river, with Omdurman on the western bank. The traffic jam on the bridge was even heavier than other parts of city. We made a tortoise movement through the one lane bridge to the other side, which is el-Mogran in Khartoum, a green recreational area at the confluence of the Blue and White Nile.

The traffic flow became easier and smooth. We drove faster through the cleaner and better lit streets of Khartoum to the Amarat suburb where the airport was. We arrived at the airport four hours earlier than the mandatory time required on the tickets. The taxi driver offered to stay with me for a while, but I declined. He helped me with my small bag to the departure gates, which were shut.

As we hugged goodbye, I became emotional and promised to myself to write every friend I had, the moment I arrived Nigeria. The cab driver asked whether it was my first time to leave the country and showered me with advice of dos and don'ts once I arrived in that strange country. With that, he got back in his cab and drove off. I was alone wil my bag.

I walked up to the departure gates. It was an unusually cold morning. A man in uniform appeared and gave me an enquiring look. I told him that I was headed for Nigeria and came early because I was not familiar with air travel procedures. He was surprised yet sympathetic and beckoned me inside the building to wait. I found myself in a wide hall with weighing machines and counters. The man pointed to a long bench at one end.

I sat down, feeling the anxiety which comes to the first time air traveler. I reached in my bag for an old novel from an African writer's series which I was reading. After about an hour, other travelers began arriving.

The Sudan Airways ticket counter opened and good looking women in smart outfits began checking in passengers.

After I was issued my boarding pass, a man in a Sudan Airways uniform asked me to step into an adjoining office. Two stern looking security officers in civilian dress were inside. One of them looked through my passport, asking questions why I was traveling to Nigeria. I was nervous as I replied, praying silently that he would let me through. Finally, he handed back my passport and with a brief smile wished me a safe journey.

It was seven o'clock in the morning when the boarding announcement was made. On the plane I was seated next to two young gentlemen. These were men I met when I went to the Nigerian consulate to obtain my visa. One of them, named Eisa was in a suit and tie, while the other, Suliman, was in West African attire. They were from Chad but lived in Sudan and occasionally in Nigeria. I conversed with them throughout the three and half hours flight across Western Sudan and Chad. I was glad to be around people who were experienced travelers and knew their way around the different countries.

Our plane landed at the Kano International Airport in Kano city, the capital of the Kano state in Northern Nigeria. As I stepped off the aircraft on that morning of February 24th, 1982, I breathed in the smell of a new land, new weather, and the start of a new life.

We were beckoned by an official to line up. I was amazed that women joined the same line as the men, because in Sudan – and Khartoum, for that matter - it is strictly forbidden for men to be in the same line with women.

I was also struck by the difference between the Khartoum and Kano airports, between the people in Sudan and Nigeria, both in dress and language, though they had the same features. People seemed less gender conscious than in Sudan. Almost all the men wore voluminous, flowing robes with elaborate embroidered collars and a *hulana* cap. The women wore either long dresses or two piece outfits, with head coverings and what looked like half a Sudanese *tobe*. These stark differences made me feel that I really was in a foreign land and a strange society.

After getting through immigration, I searched for my two friends from Chad. I met them arguing with the immigration officers. Neither had an entry visa to Nigeria, but had hoped to buy their way in. The argument wasn't about why they came to the country without visas, but rather on how much should they pay to get their passports stamped for entry. They haggled back and forth with the officers before paying an amount well over the visa fee at the embassy and finally gained entry.

As we walked out of the terminal, Eisa and Suliman told me they were going to stay for a day or so at a Chadian friend's house in the city before proceeding for the town where they expected their cattle to arrive for market. They asked me to join them and, since I did not know where else to go, accepted their invitation.

We caught a cab and sped toward the city through heavy traffic, mostly of motor bikes and commuter mini buses. The countless motor bikes, some with more than two riders, cut us off both sides with lots of hooting and shouting, heedless of the danger. The vehicles were mostly French and in better condition than the ones in Khartoum. The closer to the city we got, the more the traffic and crowds grew and the slower we moved.

Along the street sides there were hawkers of all sorts of goods calling on top of their voices to attract attention. They ran from one vehicle to another, thrusting their items through the windows of the vehicles in hopes of making sales.

We arrived at a slum with a bazaar filled with people. Refuse was littered every where. "This is Sabon Gerry," explained one of my friends. They directed the driver to the house of their friend, named Alhaji Ali. The house had a large front yard and a praying area which was clearly marked.

After paying the driver, we entered what appeared to be the guest quarters. Instead of furniture, there were plastic mats and pillows on the floor. A middle-aged man wearing an old Hausa dress dozed there. As we entered the room, he awoke and hurried to help with the luggage, exchanging greetings in Hausa with my friends, who addressed him as Alhaji Sani. They gave him some money and he disappeared, returning shortly with bottles of cold soda drinks and accompanied by another man carrying on his head a large metal bowl covered with sheets of wrapping paper.

The other man turned out to be roasted meat seller. He brought out large chunks of dark roasted meat from his bowl and my friends bargained with him for the price. They bought a portion, which the man cut it to small pieces with some onions on a piece of an old newspaper. My friends eagerly started to eat, but I hesitated. I had never seen meat roasted and carried around and sold in a dirty looking piece of newspaper. I asked myself" What kind of meat it it? is it healthy? is it safe to eat?" I asked Eisa what type of meat was it. He seemed surprised by my question. "Livestock meat, of course! What else could it be?" I didn't ask any more questions and I was hungery. I took a bite and it tasted good and we ate it all, down to the last piece of onion.

My friends then decided after some rest that it was best for them to leave immediately to conduct their business, as their cattle might have already arrived in the town of Maiduguri in the far northeast of the country, and the following day was the town's market day for cattle. They assured me that Alhaji Ali was a good man and a brother, that he would be of help to me if I needed, and I shouldn't worry about being alone in a strange country for the first time.

They tried to give me some Nigerian money. I refused at first in a show of Sudanese magnanimity, but they insisted, saying it was just for my cigars and a token of friendship, since we never knew where or when we would meet again. And in any case, I needed it, because I had yet to exchange any of my money into the local currency.

Bidding me farewell, they left for the station with Alhaji Sani escorting them. For the first time I was alone in my new country. In the evening, Alhaji Sani returned but we could not communicate well as he only spoke Hausa and very little Arabic in a Chadian dialect and surprisingly no English.

A little while, Alhaji Ali came in. He was a tall man of Arab or Fulani mulatto complexion in his mid to late forties. I exchanged greetings with him. He spoke slowly in Chadian Arabic dialect, but I had no difficulty understanding him. I explained how I ended up at his home with friends and inquired about Adam Shugar. He said he knew Shugar but not where he lived or worked. Other than that, he seemed in no mood to talk. Later we were joined by more people and after the evening meal and prayer, Alhaji left without saying good night.

The following morning I resolved to search for my cousin Shugar. Though it was still early morning, just a little after the sunrise, the streets were crowded with all sorts of people and vehicles, motor bikes and bicycles.

I hailed a taxi cab and to my relief, the driver spoke English. I asked him if he knew the location of the School of Arabic and Islamic Studies. He was not sure of the exact location but assured me that it would not be a problem. I got in the cab, where his car stereo was playing the music of Bob Marley. I felt uplifted as the Reggae legend sang *Stand up, get up for your rights.*

After asking directions from another cab driver, we drove to what looked like a middle class suburb, and stopped in front of the gate of a school. An elderly man was sitting on a bench inside the iron gate. I came out of the taxi and mentioned Adam Shugar's name and we were directed to another school, the School of Islamic and Legal Studies. We drove in the opposite direction to the outskirts of the city.

At the gate again I enquired about Adam Shugar. The gate man assured me that he works there and directed me to one of the staff rooms. I paid the the driver and headed to the offices, where I met a number of classical Arabic speaking Nigerians staff members who were not too eager to talk. After a while I was approached by a Middle Eastren man. He shook my hand and introduced himself as Kasim. He said he could take me to Shugar's house in his car.

Kasim was a lecturer of Iraqi origin in Shugar's school, he drove to what appeared to be a new housing estate. The houses were modern style and beautiful, the streets relatively clean. We stopped in front of a one story building which had two separate entrances. Kasim pointed out to the upper part of the building as Shugar's residence. I thanked him with a hand shake and picked up my bag, then walked round into a spacious subterranean back yard.

In the yard there were a number of people squatting and sitting on a large mat. Their faces looked familiar but before I could greet them, I heard my name. As I came closer, everyone stood up to welcome me. Immediately I recognized one of them, Omda. He was an old school mate. It turned out that they were all Zaghawas from my own area. I felt like I had come home. We exchanged the usual warm Zaghawa and Sudanese greetings, then they led me upstairs where there were more people. It was a truly brotherly atmosphere. I asked about Shugar but was told he just left for his work at the school.

I was pleasantly surprised to meet so many of my own people in Kano, a place where I thought I might not meet anyone who would recognize me apart from Shugar, but it turned out to be home away from home. We exchanged stories of how each one of us came to Kano, and they were eager to hear about home.

All of them came from Libya en route to Sudan, after working for a while in that country. Each wanted to buy a used Japanese Nissan UD truck, which was popular in Sudan at the time, and the main vehicle of long distance transportation for both passengers and goods. In Zaghawa parlance, having a Nissan UD truck in those days was like having a guarantee for a good life and wealth. It was both a sign of wealth and prestige and had taken over the place of camels or herds, hence Zaghawa traders and immigrant workers in Libya dreamed of buying these used trucks in Nigeria.

It also turned out that these Zaghawas in Shugar's home were among the first, if not the first ever, pioneers of commercial activity between Sudan and Nigeria, which later spread across Chad and the Central African Republic. By the twenty-first century, it had become a multi-million dollar annual trade. Shugar's pivotal role in this cannot be over-emphasized.

As we drank sodas and talked, Shugar arrived. A man of an average height and size, although in his mid thirties, he was balding from the front to the back of his head. Even though we met several times before in Sudan and were acquainted with each other fairly well, we never had an opportunity to be close. He was from a generation of venerated early Zaghawa graduates of the mid-seventies, when graduates were very few. I was of his younger brother's generation. He greeted me warmly with a truly brotherly disposition. He had received news of my arrival from his colleagues at the school and decided to come back to meet me. I felt humbled by this gesture.

We spent the rest of the day sipping warm, sweetened tea and conversing about the domestic affairs of Sudan. While some also played cards, Shugar played chess. In the evening Shugar suggested I accompany him to a visit to a friend of his in the city. Our outing turned out to be a memorable one. In addition to visiting his friend Hassan Malik who worked with the Saudi Arabian Consulate, he also took me to several places in the city - tourist attractions, restaurants, and hotels. It was late by the time we returned home.

The next morning we had tea with omelets and bread for breakfast, prepared by one of the young men, then Shugar got ready to go to work and asked me to accompany him. Shugar was a friend to everybody at the school, lecturers and students alike. He introduced me to the principal, Alhaji Sani, a partly Sudan-educated Hausa man who spoke classical Arabic with a heavy accent. Though Nigerian, he admired every thing Sudanese, from culture to education and especially Sudanese music. When he learned that I was fresh from Khartoum, he was delighted and spoke of his days at the University of Khartoum, where he earned his masters degree. He extended an invitation for us to lunch with him the following day at his family's house in the old city.

Days and weeks passed and our outings became a daily routine. So were the card and chess games in our spare time. We were young and full of youthful tendencies and romantic frolics; we appreciated good food, especially roasted meat or chicken; and admired beautiful ladies.

It was common in those days to see on the streets, especially at the entrances of major hotels and restaurants, prostitutes from different nationalities from west Africa. We pitied their misery and degregation, wondering what circumstances would force a virtuous woman to sell herself in the streets and why their families or even their governments and government of Nigeria would allow it on its streets.

CHAPTER FOUR

$\mathcal{T}$he Chad Turmoil and Zaghawa in Politics

Until coming to Nigeria, I never felt connected to what was going on in Chad in the late seventies and eighties, mainly because at the time the primary actors in the conflict were not Beri or Zaghawa. They were the Southern Sara ruling elites pitched against the FROLINAT fighters of the Northern Chad tribes who were mainly of Quran and Tobo ethnicity, led by Gukuni Wedeye and Hissein Habré. Until the Habré's government take over in August 1983, very few Zaghawas occupied prominent positions in politics and government.

Some of the important political names we used to hear in Sudan were Abbo Nassor Abdulla Borgo and Captain Mahmoud Abdul Rahman Hagar, from the Kobe ruling family of Hereba. The former was prominent politician who served in various ministerial positions in the government of Ngarta Tombalbaye, while Captain Hagar was a military officer who took part in the coup which over threw Tombalbaye in 1976 and brought Malome to power. He was assassinated during what was known in Chad as, "The Battle of Nine Months," between Gukuni Wedeye's forces of FAB, supported by Libyans and Habré's forces of FAN. These were largely composed of Zaghawa commanders and fighters, prominent among them commanders such as Ibrahim Hitno, Hassan Jamous, and Idriss Déby.

Even among these names, I was familiar only with the former two until coming to Kano. It was through Shugar, who had come to Nigeria through Chad, that I got a better picture of the Zaghawa position and involvement in the Chad Politics. I realized that our Chad brethren did better in the politics of their country than we did in Sudan.

By the time I came to Kano, the Chadian problem was at cross roads. Hissein Habré was defeated and nearly killed the previous year in the nine month battle of N'Djamena and fled to Sudan. Rumor had it that he escaped death or capture with the help of the Zaghawa fighters in his army. In 1982, he was preparing to set up training camps in Darfur for a counter-offensive against GUNT in N'Djamena. One thing that was a source of concern for us was the presence of Beri fighters on both sides of the conflict.

We spent almost every evening discussing the situation in Sudan and Chad, especially the Chad problem and its impact on Darfur and the Zaghawa. We were disgusted by many issues, particularly that of the role played by Colonel Gaddafi and Nemairy on the destabilization of Chad. Those discussions were instrumental to the future roles and careers we followed.

Shugar made friends with the Chadian community in Kano and during our visits to Sudanese friends we often took time to visit some of these Chadians. Those visits later proved useful and fruitful on personal level. It was during these visits that we met Shugar's beautiful wife, Hajia Fanania. She was a women of rare generosity and ingenuity on how to make a living. In the later days, Fanania proved to be an asset to both of us.

The three months I spent in Kano with Shugar cemented our relationship to the extent that we felt like real brothers. There was complete transparency to our relationship. We shared personal items, from cigarettes to clothing and money.

Both of us worked toward finding a job for me in Kano, which by then was becoming more difficult to get, and even if there was one to be found, it would not pay as well as it used to. Nigerian currency was losing value daily. From almost two Naira to one American dollar at the time of my arrival to Kano, it depreciated to less than fifty cents to a Naira. Even with Shugar's salary, which was considered on the high side of the Nigerian salary scale, it became more and more difficult to maintain our style of living.

This was at a time when the stream of visitors from Sudan to Kano was at its peak. Shugar tried to supplement his income through other business efforts, using his contacts with both the Sudanese and Chadian communities. We also explored all his friendly relationships and contacts to get a job for me. At this point, things became so frustrating that I seriously reconsidered whether I did the right thing by coming to Nigeria. Even more tormenting were the letters I received from my brother Eshaq in Sudan concerning the family living conditions in Fashir.

I finally suggested to Shugar if it would be a good idea for me to leave Nigeria for Libya, but he insisted that I should be patient, that things would work out to improve the situation, and that some how our two destinies were connected. As far as he was concerned, the two of us would stand by each other. He pointed out that opportunities in Nigeria were far better than in any Arab country to further my education and that he would be of help if I needed. I was deeply touched by his generous spirit. Not even brothers of the same parents showed such feelings of brotherly love. In return, I promised to be by his side in his hour of need.

CHAPTER FIVE

New Life in Lagos

It turned out that Lagos and not Kano was the land of opportunity for me. I was offered an appointment as a translator at the Saudi Arabian cultural attaché's office there. Again Shugar and his network of friends played a major role in landing me that job. A good friend of his named Mohamed Haj Elnour who worked at the Saudi Arabian consulate in Kano was the connection and link to the Saudis. Even though I loved and wished to live and work in Kano I had to relocate to Lagos, and I prepared myself for it. At the time of my departure Both Shugar and I realized that we had very little money.

Intending to locate vehicles shipped from Europe to Nigeria, two friends, Abdallah Ali and Tahir Gasi who were guests of Shugar, decided to take a trip to Lagos with me. We intended to be guests and lodge with a Darfuri expatriate and business man named Kamal who had been living in Lagos for several years and managed a shipping company of a wealthy Sudanese businessman in Kano. I had doubts that the man would be friendly to our cause, but Shugar suggested that we should just go to his house in the spirit of Sudanese and Darfuri brotherhood and pray that he would be receptive.

Shugar drove us to the *Tashan Lagos*, or Lagos bus station, and remained with us until it was time to leave. The bus station was crowded like any other bus station of a major Nigerian city. There were hawkers of merchandise and food, shoe polishers, nail cutters, touts, and beggars.

Even children as young as eight or nine were hawking items. It was heart breaking to see these children in the market.

Though the place was called a bus station, various vehicles of different sizes parked there looking for passengers through touts, or agents who called on top of their voices for passengers. There were four seat cars, twelve seat mini buses, and larger buses with around fifty seats. Each had its own price and trip time to Lagos. The smaller ones were faster and reached Lagos sooner and were therefore more expensive. Since we had little money, we opted for the larger bus. Despite our dwindling supply of cash, we were young, full of enthusiasm, and expected the best was yet to come.

As the bus sounded its horn to signal its departure, we climbed on board, jostling for seats along with the other passengers. There was no assigned seating, so we sat together side by side on one row of very small, tight seats. The bus sped through the busy street and we passed through several small towns before stopping briefly at Kaduna, a major Northern city.

Though it was night, I could discern the beauty of the country side. We passed from what seemed to be light vegetation into rich, thick forests. By mid night we reached Ilorin, the half way between Kano and Lagos and also the beginning of Yoruba land, one of the three major ethnic groups which form Nigeria. We stepped off the bus to stretch our legs and get some fresh air.

Unlike the bus stations in Sudan, there were no tea and coffee shops nor restaurants. Instead there were "Soya" meat sellers, women selling what seemed like junk food out of large cooking pots or bowls. There were also fruit sellers of mainly oranges and bananas. Since we had little money, we skipped this meal. Despite our poor circumstances, we were in a light mood, sharing stories and cracking jokes.

At dawn we drove into the city of Ibadan. We continued on ward journey for about an hour until some one said we are in Lagos. We finally reached the bus station, where the driver shouted, "Iddo, final destination!" We had arrived.

We stood discussing our next move when Tahir said we should head directly to the Kamal's house. We walked for about an hour until we reached a one story building with a small fenced yard in front. The gate was open, so we entered and knocked on the door. There was no answer.

After banging on the door several times, the door was opened by a woman who looked unfriendly. She asked whom we wanted; when we mentioned Kamal, Tahir pushed his way in and to our surprise, the woman gave way. We entered a nicely furnished living room. The woman rushed in without a word and did not come back. We sat on the comfortable sofas and waited for Kamal or anyone to emerge from the rooms and greet us, but no one appeared for a long time. Eventually a man of Northern Sudanese extraction named Mahjub came out, greeting us with a drunkard's smile. He was hung over. After a while another fellow came out of the room where the woman had disappeared. He was smoking and equally as hung over as the first man. He sat down beside us and introduced himself as Alzein. He did not speak a word for a long time after that and continued smoking, the fumes filling the air. Tahir, a devout Muslim boardering to fanaticism, grew uncomfortable and restless.

When Tahir asked him of Kamal, he replied that Kamal had traveled to Port Hartcourt, the Nigerian oil city. After a while, the woman left the house and we realized who she really was. I could sense Tahir praying silently to God to save him from sin and impurity.

We learned that both men were sailors who worked on ocean liner commercial ships. It was my first time to see a sailor, an occupation I had only read about in English literature. They were not like the sailors depicted in *Treasure Island* by Robert Louis Stevenson, though I didn't doubt that sea life was a tough life for both men.

We spent a miserable night there. Swarms of loud, humming mosquitoes flew in through the torn nets on the windows. We took turns fanning and blowing away the insects, we also took turns one person sleeping while the other two blew away the flying tormentors until day break, when the mosquitoes disappeared in to dark corners.

That morning we explained our mission in Lagos to Mahjub and Alzein. Mahjub volunteered to accompany me to the cultural attaché office since he knew Sudanese who worked there.

We hailed a taxi cab and got on our way through the congested streets. I was struck by the level of progress and development of the city. There were more by pass and over head bridges than I could count. Our Sudan capital of three cities of Khartoum, Omdurman and Khartoum North in Sudan had only three bridges at the time.

I was amazed to discover how ignorant the Sudanese about the state of development of other African countries, especially Nigeria. In Sudan, Nigerians were called *Fallata*, viewed as less than equal and looked down upon them by the Jallabas. No Sudanese I knew was aware that the so-called *Fallata* had a country and a capital far larger and prettier than Khartoum.

Two hours later we arrived at the cultural attaché's office. At the reception desk I introduced myself and the purpose of my visit and was immediately ushered into the attaché's office. His name was Sheikh Abdelaziz. He sat behind a large mahogany desk, guarded on each side by Nigerian Muslim Sheikhs with head covers which resembled the Saudi style.

Sheikh Abdelaziz was a white Arab, whiter than any Arab I have ever seen. He appeared a pious sheikh in every respect, from his complete attire of a Saudi mullah to his huge, long beard, which showed signs of faded dyeing. He welcomed me in and offered me Arabic coffee, then took me on a tour of the building, showing me various offices and introducing me to the staff.

We ended the tour in a room with large book shelves and a desk. It was to be my office. Sheik Abdelaziz filled me in on the job specifics and the monthly salary. I accepted the job, which was to start the following day. I planned to spend the rest of the day looking for housing, but the Sheikh solved that problem: there was a room I could use within the embassy for the moment.

That afternoon we all converged at Kamal's place. Abdalla and Tahir also had a productive day: they had visited the port with Alzein to find the vehicles they had imported from Europe.

The following morning I woke up early and prepared for my new job. I also agreed with Abdalla and Tahir that they should stay at Kamal's place until I could solve our financial problem with the help of my new friends at the Saudi office.

My first day on the job went smoothly. I did few translations and interpretations for the Sheikh and helped the other staff. I discovered my new living quarters was furnished with a bed and mat. I borrowed money from the Sheikh to give myself, Tahir and Abdallah something to live on. The Sheikh agreed to deduct it from my salary at the end of the month.

After two months on the job, I became exposed to the Nigerian Muslim leadership community, especially the Lagos area Muslim community. These Muslim leaders - imams, alfas, teachers, missionaries and other learned men of Islamic faith - came to the Saudi cultural attaché's office, which was virtually an Islamic learning center for guidance on Islamic spiritual issues and for financial assistance for their schools and missionary work. Most did not speak classical Arabic very well, so I served as an interpreter between them and Sheikh Abdelaziz.

I became acquainted with men who were highly placed in their communities for their combination of religious knowledge and material wealth, men such as Aziz Arisikola, a wealthy business man and Yuroba Muslim leader, and the late MKO Abiola, an international business tycoon who ran for president in 1994 and won, but was denied the position by the Nigerian military ruler.

It was during these visits when I became acquainted with Alhaj Hussein Mohammad, a graduate of Al-Azhar Islamic University in Egypt and an imam of a large mosque in a Lagos suburb. He was also a broadcaster with the Radio Nigeria Arabic Service. Alhaj Hussein introduced me to the broadcasting field and offered me an evening job, so I started working with Radio Nigeria Arabic Service in June 1982 while maintaining my day job with the Saudi office. As Shugar rightly predicted things began to work out well in Lagos.

I also developed the habit of visiting their mosques, especially during Friday prayer times, to know more about the islamised Yuroba culture. It was then I discovered that Islam in Yuroba land had completely Africanized. At some mosques in Lagos, Islam drew closer to African Christianity or the African way of worshiping and observing rituals. Rumors abounded that some learned men of Muslim faith combined both Islamic and Christian teachings in their mosques. There were also known instances of imams converting to Christianity and pastors converting to Islam. Many Yurobas were said to be attending both Sunday church prayers and Friday mosque prayers.

It was a unique case for religious tolerance and the philosophic understanding of the human way of life and relationship to God. At the time I thought perhaps that was why the Yuroba society was among the most sophisticated and organized among African societies. I was bemused by the way the prayer setting was organized at Alhaji Hussien's mosque, and by the way he led the Friday prayer, and by the clapping, singing and dancing which followed. Within the prayer area there was no clear separation between where the females sat and prayed and where the men sat and prayed. This bore some similarity to a church setting or an African shrine setting. The singing and clapping of hands also reminded me of African gospel music sung in churches.

CHAPTER SIX

$\mathcal{N}$igeria Expels Illegal Aliens

After eight months working with the Saudis and Radio Nigeria Arabic Service, the deteriorating economic conditions in the West African country reached a crisis point. The democratic government of President Shehu Shagari battled rising inflation and the dwindling purchasing power of the Naira. Nigerian currency lost value almost daily. Workers in both the public and private sectors found it more and more difficult to make a living. Crime rate was on the rise, especially in the major cities of the South. Roadside armed robbery with loss of lives and late night house break-ins by the armed robbers became common, along with rumors of corruption in high government circles.

Many Nigerians believed the huge immigrant population in the country, of which the Ghanaians formed the majority, was mostly to blame for the sudden down turn of the economy. The government of Shehu Shagari, which was facing an election year, was desperate to salvage the situation before the election in August 1984.

By November 1982, the Shagari government gave in to public opinion and made a complete U-turn to its declared foreign policy objectives. The government declared that foreigners, or, to be precise, "illegal aliens" were behind economy's down turn and the crime waves suffered by the southern parts of the country. Under pretext of national security and soveriety of the Nigerian state, the government gave those who were staying and working in the country without residence permits thirty days either to regularize their stay or leave. No exceptions were made for nationalities, which was viewed by some observers as an infringement to the treaties and agreements that established the Economic Community of West African States (ECOWAS).

Ghanaians, who formed the bulk of undocumented immigrants, took this decision as directed solely at them. They left immediately with the assistance of their home government, a thing which amazed the Nigerian authorities. Within days, hundreds of thousands of Ghanaians left Nigeria for Ghana, in what was described by some observers at the time, as the greatest human exodus in African history.

The Nigerian government decision put me in some difficulty. I was living and working in the country on a visitor's visa which had to be renewed every three months, and I had been doing it for over a year. It became imperative to upgrade to a work visa. Also at this time, the Saudi Embassy wanted to transfer my services from the cultural attaché office to the Embassy itself to be its official translator.

Application was made by the Embassy to the Nigerian Foreign Affairs ministry requesting a change of status for me from visitor to resident working for the Embassy, but the ministry said a work visa must be granted from a Nigerian Embassy abroad, thus I had to leave the country and reenter with a work visa.

The Embassy made arrangements for me to travel to Saudi Arabia in company of an official, Mohammad Hassan, who was also traveling on a mission for the Saudi foreign ministry, to obtain my visa from the Nigerian Embassy in Jeddah. We traveled to Kano to catch a Saudi Airlines flight to Jeddah the following day.

In Kano I lodged with Shugar, a home away from home. While there I met some Chadian friends who fled the violent take over of Hissein Habré a few months earlier. Just like old times, our discussions centered on the politics of our country and Chad, continuing until late in the night.

The next day, I went to the airport with Shugar and other friends. At the departure gate I bade them farewell. The flight to Jeddah took about four and a half hours. We landed at the best and most modern airport terminal I had ever seen up until that time.

Friends of Mohammad Hassan met us there - jovial, easy-going young Saudi Arabs. Despite their friendliness and sense of humor, it was apparent that I was a complete stranger to the land and the people.

They were completely different in terms of culture and race from the Africans, especially West Africans. Despite the semi-mosaic appearance the immigrant population stamped on the place, the majority here were Arabs, men in traditional long white garments, head scarves and gear, women hidden in black hijabs with nothing seen of their bodies, not even their faces. There were some exceptions of foreign women whose faces were uncovered. It was clear that this was a male-dominated society where women had very little role in deciding its affairs.

I wondered who I knew in this country and remembered that I had a cousin, Rajab Ebra, who lived and worked in Jeddah for several years, but I had never met him and had no contact with him, besides the fact that it was the middle of the night with little chance of finding any Sudanese who could take me to him. I did not think of going to a hotel.

Mohammad Hassan interrupted my thoughts, insisting that I be his guest for the night at Makkah, "the holiest of the Muslim holy places on earth." I accepted his offer eagerly. The Mohamed Hassan and his friends were a nice group of fellows, and despite our racial and cultural differences, I felt at ease with them.

In Makkah, Hassan's house was composed of two sections, the men's section and a harem's section. I was ushered into a simple Arab-style living room and spent the rest of the night alone. Early the following morning, Hassan appeared from the inner rooms, still in his previous night pajamas, with a huge tray of food and beverages for breakfast.

After breakfast, Hassan drove us to the Embassy, where we were well received by the Nigerian Ambassador, Alhaji Waziri, and his staff. As we sipped tea in the ambassador's office, Hassan explained why I needed a work visa. Waziri was hesitant and reminded us of the latest measures taken by the Nigerian government on immigration and immigrants to the country. He requested us to wait several weeks until the disruption created by the expulsion of the illegal immigrants died down.

His position was understandable, although Hassan felt slighted,and refused to accept it. He reminded the Ambassador about a work visa he granted to Ambassador's driver to come and work for him in Saudi Arabia,and demanded resiprocity. The Ambassador said he is aware of that but needed some time to grant my visa. We left the Embassy without the visa, though Hassan promised to go back to Nigeria and exert pressure from there to accelerate the process. I was to remain in Jeddah.

We started to look for my cousin in hopes he could help me stay on in the city. Eventually we met fellow Darfuris who knew him and directed us to him. My cousin Rajab lived in the Bab Sharif suburb of Jeddah, and, as customary in Sudanese communities abroad, he shared a house with many young Sudanese, mostly of riverine extraction. He was the same age with me, though the strict religious life of Saudi had taken its toll on him. He grew a huge beard,prayed the five times at the mosque,and was very pious.

During the time, I was given the best brotherly treatment ever. I spent several memorable weeks with him before I finally got my visa to return to Nigeria.

CHAPTER SEVEN

Return to Nigeria

In route to return to Nigeria, I decided to pass through Chad to have first-hand knowledge about the country and the Zaghawa presence in its government, especially after Habré took over power some months earlier with the help of Zaghawa fighters. I changed my Saudi Airline ticket to Sudan Air which flies from Jeddah to N'Djamena via Khartoum.

On the plane, I sat next to a Chad resident of mixed Sudanese Nigerian parentage, Alhaji Suliman, who was returning to N'Djamena after performing a Lesser Haj, or pilgrimage, in Saudi Arabia. Throughout the four hour flight to N'Djamena, we spoke mostly about Chadian politics, though he detested what he termed the acrimonious and bloody tribal politics of Chad. His conversation revealed that he was a die-hard supporter of Hissein Habré's FAN organization, and believed that Hissein Habré, as a French educated politician, could bring effective change and development to the war-torn country, if only stability could be achieved.

After I learned where he stands politically, I did not disclose much of my political leanings; I was well aware that Sudanese and Chadian intelligence services worked closely those days. He, too, cautioned me not to talk much on politics if I intend to spend time in N'Djamena.

Once we arrived in N'Djamena, he learned I had no specific place to lodge in the town but intended to find a hotel then proceed to Nigeria by road. He showed the customary Chadian generosity and insisted that I stay with him in his house for the rest of the day and leave the following morning. It was an agreeable offer, which I received with some reservation, but in the end I obliged.

We disembarked from the plane to a terminal building which looked like an old hospital or school building. The officials were unidentifiable from the rest of people, wearing no distinguishable uniform which identified them from the rest. There were no luggage conveyors or counters for officials, as in other international air ports. Everything was handled manually by men who looked some how very polite. The furniture was either in tatters or very old.

Outside the terminal, we saw a few old taxi cabs and hailed one. On the way to his house, I could see the scars of war on the walls of the buildings in what used to be a nice, beautiful town. Many houses were either destroyed or their walls riddled with bullet holes. The taxi cab drove through what seemed to be the only well-paved major street in the city, the "Charles de Gaulle," where houses on both sides looked beautiful but scarred, reminders of the ferocious battles which took place there. Later I learned from Alhaji Suliman that those were government buildings inherited from the Colonial Era.

We proceeded to the suburbs, where there were no tarred roads and the houses were of middle or lower class, until we reached Alhaji Suliman's house. It was a huge compound with many brick and mud rooms divided by walls. We were greeted by his wives and children and I was taken to a guest room with two beds and mats on the floor. Moments later, Alhaji's neighbors also trooped in to greet him.

There were many cultural similarities between the Sudanese, especially of Darfur, and the Chadians. I felt almost amongst Darfuris, and when the food was served, which was brought in from both Alhaji's house and the neighbors', it was the same food of Darfur - the *Asida* millet porridge with *Tagalia* stew. I felt these people were even closer to Darfur people than the riverine Sudanese.

Alhaji and the neighbors stayed with me in the guest room until night. We conversed on diverse issues, but talked little of politics, until the call for prayer was made. After prayer, I was left alone in the room. Before going to sleep, I reflected on how to make some contacts in the town the following morning before my departure to Nigeria.

The next day, after having tea and breakfast with Alhaji, I inquired whether it would be possible to visit some of the government officials from the Beri or Zaghawa, but he discouraged me, saying they were too preoccupied with their new responsibilities and that they hardly had the time or attention for someone like me who spoke no French but heavily accented Sudanese Arabic and Zaghawa. In any case, entries to most government offices were manned by people from Quran, Habré's own tribe, and Chadians feel affronted when spoken to in a Sudanese accent. I saw the wisdom in his logic and decided to defer the immediate contacts; instead I went out to get a good feeling of the town, which reminded me of my own town Alfashir.

I walked through the streets and felt an overwhelming sense of poverty, real poverty. I also realized that there were few children on the streets, indicative that few families lived there, as many had fled the war and crossed the border to Cameroon and Nigeria. My walk lasted for several hours, during which I visited the main market, which looked in every respect like a Darfuri town market. The merchandise on the shop shelves, especially fabrics, looked dusty, as if they had been there for a long time, an indication that sales were slow. Although at several places I came across groups of people who spoke Zaghawa language with a Chad Kobe accent, I did not venture to speak with any of them.

It was late afternoon before I returned to Alhaji Suliman's house, and again Alhaji advised that if I had any plan of leaving for Nigeria that evening, I should delay it until the following morning, as it would be good to cross the borders during the day.

In the morning Alhaji gave me a ride to the border on his motorcycle, the "Mobolet," as they call it in N'Djamena. A few yards from the Chari River border post, which was on low ground and could hardly be seen from a distance, he stopped and explained to me that it would be good for him if he did not go near to the officials, as they would look for financial gain out of him.

I bade him farewell and carried my two bags to a building close to the river mouth. As I approached the building, I could see a crowd near the river, along with canoes. Some were crossing the river to and fro, while some laid in wait. The officials wore no distinguishable uniforms, just like at the airport, but they did wear huge turbans which covered both the head and the chin.

I approached one of them and gave him my passport. It was then I realized that he could neither read Arabic nor English and I doubted if he could read French at all. He held the passport upside down and looked at it and began asking in Chad Arabic questions like when did I enter Chad and where was I headed. I answered all his questions regardless of the fact that he could find the answers in the passport. Another official harshly ordered me to open my bags. They searched every corner and opened every item and in the end asked me to pay two thousands CFA francs to cross. I hired a canoe and crossed to the other side of the river.

As I came out of the canoe, I spotted more officials in immaculate uniforms, seated in chairs under a tree not far from the river. The stark contrast between the dress of the officials on this side of the river and the ones on the other side surprised me. I passed them by to where I could see a town and vehicles. It did not occur to me that they were actually Cameroonian officers on border post, and the place was Kosouri, a border town.

I reached what seemed to be a traveler's departure station where there were various kinds of vehicles of different sizes. Still laboring under the belief that I would get my entry visa, I paid for a mini bus ticket and embarked on an uncomfortable journey in a vehicle packed with passengers. The bus moved out of the town on a dusty road, kicking up huge clouds of dust behind it.

After an hour or so our vehicle was stopped by two officers on motor bikes mounting a road block. They ordered all men in the vehicle to disembark. They went through the travel documents of each person and ordered each to pay one thousand CFA francs. When it was my turn, I was ordered to pay two thousands because according to them, I had no entry visa. Only then I realized that I was actually in Cameroon without a visa.

The journey continued and thereafter I was made to pay two thousands at every road block, of which there were four. Finally we reached the town of Gambaro at the Nigerian border. At the border exit I was ordered to pay five thousands for the same reason. They also insisted that was the entry fee charged at Kosouri. I objected and tried to explain to their superior my ordeal, but he gave me the ugly option of going back to Kosouri to have my entry visa stamped, only then he wouldn't ask me a single franc.

A good Samaritan co-passenger, who seemed to be one of the locals and knew the officers, was irked by the delay caused by the argument and came to my help. He paid four thousand on my behalf, insisting they take it. The officers accepted and we proceeded through the town and to the other side of the border, where I paid him back.

At the Nigerian entry post I did not encounter any difficulties. After stamping my passport, I was assisted by an officer in getting a vehicle to Maiduguri, from where I was to catch a direct flight to Lagos or proceed to Kano.

I arrived in the city in record time, and was dropped off at the main motor park which served travelers to border areas with Cameroon, Niger and Chad. There were various types of people - traders who were busy loading all kinds of goods on trucks, hawkers young and old, and women with red teeth, which I later learned was a kind of makeup used by Borno women to make them look beautiful and attractive.

It crossed my mind that this was the place my forefathers migrated from according to the oral tradition, but I could hardly see anything Zaghawa apart from the complexion of some people. I marveled how time and geographical separation could transform people, if it was true that these people were Mahamat Bornawe's people.

As I was contemplating my next step, I heard some one calling my name. To my pleasant surprise, it was an old school mate of mine, Al Sadiq Ali Khabir, who lived and did business in the town, with another friend Salih Norain. Both were surprised to see me in a Maiduguri motor station, so I explained to them that I was returning from Saudi Arabia via N'Djamena on my way to Lagos. They insisted that I lodge with them that evening and in the morning they would assist me in hiring the best vehicle to take me to Kano in the shortest time at the least cost, and from there I could proceed to Lagos.

The idea of traveling by road from Maiduguri to Kano appealed to me, especially since I wanted to see the country side and meet Shugar in Kano if I could. By the time I agreed to their plan, they had already collected my bags and stopped a taxi. Both lived in the same house. At the house I met a number of people from Sudan. All were in town on various businesses. Sadik and Salih disappeared only to come back later with a lamb. They slaughtered the lamb and we had a roasted lamb dinner that night. I had a memorable night with them. In the morning, as he promised, Sadiq took me to the Kano motor station, where I joined three other people in a hired car to Kano.

Setting the Stage for Zaghawa Solidarity

The six hour journey to Kano was a smooth one, aside from the breath taking speed of our car and those travelling on the opposite side of the single lane road which made us engrossed and apprehensive. Upon arrival in the city, I hired a local cab to Shugar's residence. At the house, which by now was like a home, I met as usual several people in the yard; they were Zaghawa traders from Sudan and Chad.

Upstairs, I met Shugar playing a game of chess and several other people whom I did not recognize, all in Nigerian or Chadian style gowns. Shugar introduced them to me: Abas Koti, Mohammad Sabir, Mohammad Osman, and two others. They were Beri or Zaghawa brothers and friends who were prominent members of the defunct GUNT government of Chad. They were part of a larger group who survived Hissein Habré's on slaught coup and had crossed into Nigeria.

I was excited to learn that these were actually part of the Zaghawa politicians of Chad and hoped to talk with them despite the difficulties presented by our Beri and Arabic dialects. The guests, however, rarely spoke. It was apparent that Abas Koti was their leader. Mohammad Sabir was the oldest and the most verbose, speaking with a Sudanese accent in Arabic. He was born, raised, and educated in Sudan, but after a brief nursing career returned in late sixties to his extended family in Chad and later joined FROLINAT, and then the Northern Armed Forces FAB under Gukuni Wedeye.

Shugar suggested the four of us - Abas Koti, Mohammad Sabir, Shugar and myself – go out for dinner and drinks that evening. We headed to a hotel restaurant in central Kano. It was a nice European-style place with lots of Westernized folks and other Kano people. We chose to sit in a remote corner for the sake of privcy of conversation. After food and drinks were ordered, I brought up the subject of Beri solidarity and unity. To my surprise, the other three closely followed every word I said.

I began with some historical background on the Beri which I learned while reading several books on West African history - how they used to be empire builders, how their unity always achieve great things for themselves and for the rest of the African community, and how their quarrels and disunity spelled doom for them and for the region.

I started by saying that, it was a personal concern for Shugar and me to see Beri united. I emphasized the word *Beri* as a unifying word for all sections whether Wegi, Kobera, or Toba, and that their divisions along factional lines in Chad did no good for Beri and for the rest of the Chadian people. We Beri in Sudan followed these events with heavy heart, dismayed by the divisions among Beri, especially since they were the ones doing the major fighting on behalf of others who sought to establish a dynasty on behalf of a tribal elite.

My words ignited enthusiasm in the men. Mohammad Sabir was fascinated by the historical part and by the suggestion that the word *Beri* was a unifying word, though he made it clear it was not the first time he heard the idea. He explained that he had undertaken many initiatives to bring together the Beri in Chad, but failed, largely due to vested interests of certain key Beri personalities who wanted to maintain their positions,and viewed my initiative as a threat to their vested interests. Sabir did not name a particular person but was ovious whom he was referring to.

Shugar interjected, that days before my arrival, they had several meetings on the issue of unity,which included Adam Togoye, the former GUNT minister, and Sidiq Fadul, a former senior official of Qokni's administration. The later two left for Cotonou in the Republic of Benin to seek asylum there, but Shugar was asked to draft a strategy of unity for the Beri. Now that I had come back, I could also contribute to the project.

Abas Koti was the last to speak, detailing how the FROLINAT revolution was formed and how Zaghawa or Beri played significant roles in all stages. He lamented the lack of unity among Beri and believed that their unity was the solution to many problems, especially the war in Chad. He added that the Beri in Sudan could play a major role in bringing together the opposing Beri parties in Chad, just as the Beri of Chad could play a role in the solidarity of the Beri of Sudan. The purpose of their fight in Chad was to end marginalization of any group, whether through governance or other institutions. In his opinion, the unity of Beri could be the nucleus for the unity of the marginalized forces in the region.

Shugar added that what the Beri lacked was proper communication among the community and lack of clear parameters which let to the undermining of each other. In the strategy he intended to draft, efforts which lead to solidarity and unity would be promoted, beginning in Chad. Beri institutions must also be developed, with emphasis made on the education and promotion of Zaghawa commerce and trade, both within the region and internationally. In this strategy, we had to make use of the educated Zaghawas as the driving force behind the solidarity and unity we sought.

By the time we exhausted our discussion, it was late in the night. We agreed that what we discussed could not be finished in just one or even a few meetings, so we decided and affirmed to meet on a regular basis.

The cause of Beri unity, which before had been the concern of two men, had now become the concern of four men, and would later grow to seven men.

Koti and Sabir and the rest of their Chadian colleagues had been revolutionaries and prominent fighters for years against the injustice of those days. They fought with FROLINAT against a dictatorship, then again with FAB of Gukuni and won their war, but were driven out by Habré's forces - which, ironically, were commanded by Beri or Zaghawa commanders. Chief among them were Ibrahim Hitno, Hassan Jamous, Idriss Déby and others. On FAB's side there were prominent Zaghawas such as Adam Togoye, Abas Koti himself and others.

On our way back home in Shugar's vehicle, we discussed the Libyan and Sudanese involvement in Chadian political situation, along with Colonel Gaddafi's ambitions in the region. Koti and Sabir believed that although Gaddafi had his own agenda in Chad, GUNT and FAB needed Libya if they were to regain power from FAN, and that GUNT did commit a mistake by accepting an OAU decision which called for the replacement of Libyan forces by OAU forces and expelling Libyan forces from Chad. The OAU forces were in the country without a clear mandate to protect the Government of National Unity, and when Habré attacked with support from Sudan and the CIA, the OAU forces just stepped aside and watched the GUNT fall and flee the country.

We also discussed General Nemairy's interest in Habré to counter the Libyan intervention in Sudan, especially helping the opposition to his regime. We agreed that the Beri on both sides of the border were unhappy, exploited by politicians on both sides.

Early the next morning, Koti and Sabir left for Maiduguri with some of their colleagues, with promises that we would meet soon along with Togoye and Sidiq Fadul to continue our discussions. Shugar shared some of what he wrote on the strategy to unite the Beri. It was good and I offered some suggestions to be included.

That afternoon, he took me to the airport where I boarded a Nigeria Airways flight to Lagos with resolve in my heart to see the Beri unified.

CHAPTER EIGHT

Toward Beri Unity and Nigeria's Troubles

The day after I returned to Lagos, I headed to the Embassy Chancery building on Victoria Island to see the ambassador. Ambassador Fuad Mufti was an urbane gentleman and a well-polished diplomat. It was apparent that the many years he had spent abroad, especially in France, had an effect upon his outlook and lifestyle. I was well received by him, and after some enquiry about my stay in Saudi Arabia and return, he went into the details of the work he wanted me to do, which was translation of materials in English, especially media and official correspondence with the Nigerian authorities, into Arabic and vice versa.

Not long after my arrival in Lagos, Adam Togoye and Sidiq Fadul visited from Cotonou. Sidiq came to see me at the Embassy. He was a tall, lean, bearded, affable young man with a baritone voice. I accompanied him to their hotel, where I met Adam Togoye for the first time.

The much senior Togoye was an older politician with one leg hamstrung or amputated in the battles of Chad, but wore an artificial leg. Despite his disability, he was agile and walked briskly. Though Togoye was inclined to speak about the general political problem of Chad, I focused our discussion on the earlier talks I had in Kano with Shugar, Koti and Sabir on Beri unity. They agreed with all the strategies and plans.

The following day they departed for Cotonou. Cotonou was the headquarters for Chadian opposition leaders in those days because of the close relationship between the Gaddafi's revolutionary regime and the socialist regime of the Republic of Benin, headed by Mathieu Kerekou.

Some weeks later, Shugar visited me in Lagos on his way to Cotonou for further meetings with the group. I was not able to go due to work commitments, but expressed my full support to any decision which the meeting might reach.

Two days later, Shugar returned and briefed me on the outcome of the meeting. The major decision reached was that an emissary, in the person of Shugar himself, would go to N'Djamena on behalf of the group to sell the idea of Beri unity to the Beri leaders there, especially to the trio of Ibrahim Hitno, Hassan D'Jamous, and Idriss Déby. I discussed with him all the pros and cons of the matter and agreed with him the importance of the mission. We also agreed that he should start his meetings with Hitno as the most senior and less military minded in hopes that Hitno would influence the others.

Shugar traveled to N'Djamena in July 1983 and had his first and only important meeting with Hitno – by then the Minister of Interior in Habré's regime. He was well received by Hitno at his residence and held discussions with him about his mission. The result was that the group stood behind the initiative of unity of Zaghawa, and that Hitno welcomed the idea of unity of Beri, but cautioned that unity must serve the purpose of peace and rebuilding in Chad and not war and destruction. He warned that some of the names Shugar mentioned were enemies of peace, seeking to cause trouble and working with Chad's enemies against its unity and territorial integrity. Shugar as a Sudanese may be innocent, but the other Chadians with him in the project wanted to exploit it and use it against the regime.

When Shugar insisted that there was no hidden agenda against the regime and they must cooperate, Hitno countered that there could be, adding that, "The Beri are in unity or else how could some one like you, a Sudanese, go to Chad's Minister of Interior and talk of unity with the group you mentioned and be tolerated and entertained in discussion?"

This statement shocked Shugar and made him realize the vulnerability of his own situation, namely his freedom and security in a country ruled by the iron grip of a brutal dictator. He ended his meeting with Hito and immediately left Chad. Luckily for him, it only took minutes to cross to the other side of the border.

After his return, I traveled to him in Kano, where we reviewed the outcome of his visit, concluding that it was an uphill task to try to sell our idea to the Beri in power in N'Djamena, but nevertheless, we would continue our efforts.

Koti frequently traveled between the Republic of Benin, where his GUNT leadership stayed, and Maiduguri where he had his family. En route he spent time with Shugar in Kano and me in Lagos, when we reflected on the unity of the greater Zaghawa. It was a unity similar to Arab unity in the Middle East, yet not directed toward an enemy. We felt it was our right to come together after being unjustly divided a century ago by the British and French Colonial masters, and it was our duty as enlightened Beri to work to bring together the nation of Beri. We felt this could only happen through the education and enlightenment of the Beri folk, and as Shugar's strategy paper stated, the starting point must be the preservation of the Beri language – the *Beria* - its culture, and the unification and development of all Beri institutions.

We also felt that these objectives did not contradict with our national identities in the same way that Arab countries have their own various governments but still belong to the Arab League and feel they have a common destiny and a common enemy. Zaghawa unity could be an example for the unity of other ethnic nationalities in Africa divided by the Colonial system. We made this objective the purpose of our lives.

The Beri brothers in Habré's government refused to subscribe to the project for the obvious reason that they were in the government, while the main champions of the project were in the opposition.

Coup in Nigeria

By late December 1983, the economic situation of Nigeria had become more dire. The newly re-elected democratic government of Alhaji Shehu Shagari struggled with wide spread mismanagement, out of control spending on white elephant projects, and corruption in both high and low places, in addition to an astronomical rise in crime and the continued drop of Nigerian currency against major international currencies.

The government seemed uncertain how to tackle the economic situation. This affected the livelihood of both citizens and the immigrants who began to trickle in after their expulsion in December 1982. This situation also gave the military justification to take over power, thus on December 30th, 1983, Mohamdu Buhari, an army general and former official of the former military government of Olusegun Obasanjo, declared in a broadcast through national radio and television that the Nigerian army took over power from the civilian administration to stop the economic mismanagement and corruption.

I watched the lanky general on my small black and white television, announcing on the eve of the Muslim Eid festival the suspension of the constitution, the closing of Nigerian borders with neighboring countries, and the banishment of political parties, that the armed forces made up the military government, with a supreme military council and a federal executive council at the center.

I wondered whether Nigeria was heading toward socialism and communism and whether its armed forces, the only institution which was truly nationalist in character, could bury the democracy and forfeit the will of the majority of its people.

The coup dominated the headlines of Nigerian newspapers the next morning. The coup leader had special consideration for the Kingdom of Saudi Arabia, as he invited Ambassador Mufti, along with the ambassadors of the five permanent members of the security council, to a meeting with him. Although Mufti was a man of few words and showed very little of his true feelings, it was easy to see that he was delighted by the gesture of the new military strong man. He quickly made friends with the key civilian officials of the junta, especially with the Minister of Petroleum Resources. Even though he spoke English fairly well, he took me with him on most of his visits to Nigerian ministers and officials, a thing that irked his own Suadi diplomats.

Forty-eight hours into the Nigerian coup, President Jaafar Nemairy flew to Lagos to meet with the new rulers, as if to congratulate them on the success of their coup. The only explanation we could deduce at the time was that Nemairy wanted the new regime's support for Chad against Colonel Gaddafi. It was a move which surprised everyone, including the new Nigerian rulers.

The new military regime immediately took draconian measures against the former officials of the civilian administration, arresting and trying them in special tribunals, where most were given jail terms ranging from ten to two hundred years.

On the streets, most people hailed the overthrow of the Shagari government, while some groups in the North held demonstrations in support of the coup.

The Nigerian coup though could have been viewed as a relief for the country from the greed of the politicians and their cronies, but it was a set back in the evolution of democracy in Africa. We felt a deep sense of disappointment, as we considered Nigeria the leader of black Africa which held the key to the resolution of most of the continent's problems, especially the liberation of the regions still under Colonial rule, the settlement of the Chadian crisis, and the yearnings and aspirations of the marginalized in Sudan and other parts of Africa.

With the closing of the Nigerian border which lasted close to a year, the movement of members of our group became difficult. Togoye, Koti and Sidiq Fadul spent much of their time pursuing their efforts between the Republic of Benin and Libyan Arab Jamahiriya, while Sabir remained mostly in Maiduguri. Later he left for Libya. Shugar's movements became limited, as his finances were also affected by the slide of the Naira value. Thus our solidarity efforts and activities throughout 1984 went into limbo.

I maintained very close contact with Shugar and visited him regularly when I wasn't devoting much of my time to work and to the affairs of the small but organized Sudanese community in Lagos.

Throughout the two and a half years I worked with Ambassador Mufti he depended on me more than his diplomats, especially on media relations, a thing that often times put me in difficult situations with them, since they viewed his efforts as attempts to marginalize them.

Two and half years later, a new ambassador came in the person of Yahya Ahmed Al-Yahya, an easy-going man of noble origin, who would take offense himself rather than offend anybody. He preferred staying in Brazil, where he was posted from, rather than in the hustle and bustle of Lagos, a thing that irked Nigerian authorities and made them feel slighted. They often made veiled criticisms to his face, and on more than one occasion he was asked whether he is non resident Ambassador.

Though I was his employee, we became very good friends. He also followed the Mufti tradition. I was his personal translator, interpreter, advisor, and sometimes even confidant. During his seven years as ambassador, he rarely met with any high ranking Nigerian official without my presence and interpreting. Working with him and Mufti before him afforded me the exposure to foreign affairs and the diplomatic life and the world

It was during his time that I got both time and his encouragement to take corespondance courses to study for a law degree with the University of London.

When the Iraqi regime of Saddam Hussein invaded Kuwait in September 1990 and the Gulf war broke out, we bore the burden and rigors of the diplomatic and media war, in an attempt to win the Nigerian public opinion to the Kuwaiti and Saudi cause.

When Alyahya left, I was the first to feel his absence both in personal and professional terms. His successor was a sharp contrast to him, a rigid bureaucrat who was very conscious of his rank and status, yet failed to gauge the legacy bequeathed to him by his predecessors. He was not there long when things became difficult for almost everyone, especially the Sudanese staff who had enjoyed the cordial work atmosphere created by Alyahya,and Mufti before him.

In January 1996, I left my job to devote more time to our political struggle and to Beri unity, but also due to the difficult work environment.

The Solidarity Project goes into limbo

Going back to 1984,as mentioned earlier, throughout 1984 our Zaghawa solidarity activity largely became confined between Shugar and me. Around the middle of May 1984, I came to Kano on one of my usual visits to the town. By this time he was married. His marriage ceremony was so limited and private that he excluded most of his Sudanese friends, including me,not out of disregard but to avoid any kind of opposition to his marriage to his loved one. I did not hold any grudge against him,but felt happy for him. His bride accorded me all the respect known by Chadian ladies.

Shugar disclosed his intention to resign his job with the Kano Legal Islamic College and go into full time business, as his job could no longer support him, now that he is a family man. Despite my skepticism considering his lack of business experience, a sound business plan and considerable financial resources, I wished him luck. He had formed good relations with some of the wealthy people in Kano, and if his business was to utilize and invest in those contacts and relations and form a link with the Darfur trade route, there could be a good chance of success.

Not long after my return to Lagos, he and his wife left for Saudi Arabia, then to Sudan. At that time, the dictatorship of Nemairy was fifteen years in power and struggled with deteriorating economic conditions and famine which struck the Western part of the country, especially Darfur. Nemairy's intelligence and security network spread across Chad to encompass West Africa, namely Nigeria, and the Zaghawas of Sudan and Chad were under scrutiny. Even our group was suspect.

I lost contact with all the members of the solidarity group for more than a year, during which many major events shook the foundation of Sudanese politics. I was in Lagos doing my usual donkey work for the Saudi Embassy, while Shugar was in Sudan, and I had little news about him. He wrote me once telling me about the economic conditions of the country and how his own business had little success.

In April 1985, the economic conditions in Sudan became so dire. While Nemairy was on a visit to United States, the Sudanese at the center rose in revolution against him. Violent demonstrations headed by university students and trade unionists spread to cities accross the country. A military interregnum headed by general Sewar-elzahab put an end to his regime,and declared its intention to return the country to democratic rule. I followed these events zealously from Lagos.

As demonstrations and other acts of civil disobedience continued in Khartoum, I and other friends made efforts to encourage the Sudanese community in Lagos to support the uprising and its leaders. I brought together both the chairman of the community, then retired Brigadier General-turned-businessman Osman Nossor Osman, and the Secretary General of the community, Dr. Babikir Abdelsalam, to send a telegram of support on behalf of the entire community. Brigadier Osman, an experienced old military man, had reservations about the possibility that Nemairy, an old friend of his, might fall from power so fast, hence he insisted upon delaying the telegram until events took clearer shape.

Less than twenty-four hours later, the military removed Nemairy and declared an interim period of one year to prepare the country for general multi-party elections.

CHAPTER NINE

*H*omecoming

About a year after Shugar's departure from Kano, I decided to tie the knot with my long-time fiancé Hayat, and made preparations to travel to Saudi Arabia to purchase the traditional "Shaila," which is a gift bag for the bride, before returning to Alfashir in Darfur for the wedding.

I arrived in Jeddah around late June 1985 and lodged with my cousin Rajab Ibrah, who still lived and worked in the city. Rajab's generosity was immeasurable by Zaghawa standards.

It is true that Zaghawas are generous, especially with relatives from the mother's side, but it seemed one other factor also formed Rajab's generosity. He was an orphan, brought up in Omdurman by his paternal uncle Ahmed Nehar, who was famed for his generosity, and in Jeddah he lived with non-Zaghawas who were mostly from the Arabized central Sudan tribes.

Throughout the week I spent with him, he offered me all the respect for our blood relationship and friendship and assisted in every way possible. We moved through the Jeddah stores and purchased the *Shaila* items. This gesture continued each time I visited the oil rich country, even when the economy changed and things became tough for every expatriate, including Rajab.

During the first week of July, I arrived in Khartoum and to my delight met some of my best friends whom fate had separated us for years. These were none other than Shugar, Adam Harry Rahma, Salih Birish, Mohammad Bashir Abdalla and others. Adam, Salih and Mohammad were old school mates. Adam had left for Algeria for a teaching contract even before I left for Nigeria in early 1982. We had written to each other a lot but never planned to be in Khartoum at the same time. He was on vacation and heading to Alfashir.

I learned from Shugar that business was not good, especially as he found himself amidst the poverty of relatives. The previous two years were particularly bad for Darfur and people survived only on the hand outs of United States government food aid, or what was known as Reagan food aid. Politics took the better part of his time. He was busy trying to make the Darfuri voice heard in Jallaba-dominated Sudanese politics.

We reflected on our days together in Nigeria and our project of Zaghawa solidarity, reaffirming that we must continue with the effort, despite the huge differences between the N'Djamena camp and those in GUNT. Even within GUNT itself, differences appeared between Adam Togoye's group and Abas Koti's group. Shugar was willing to return to Nigeria and I agreed with him. We decided to depart together after I return from Alfashir.

The rainy season had already started, making the always difficult transportation to Alfashir from Khartoum especially difficult. A journey by road might take several days if not weeks, and air transportation was nearly impossible in my circumstances, as one has to make reservations several weeks in advanced before getting a seat in a flight by small plane to Darfur.

After about a week or so in Khartoum, luck came to my aid. My friend Adam Harry and I learned that Adam Yaakoub, a wealthy Zaghawa businessman, was chartering a small air craft to Alfashir to bring his family to Khartoum. We hurried to his office and made arrangements with his agent to get us two seats. The man charged us double the price of a normal commercial flight; nevertheless, we paid. The next morning we arrived at the airport and boarded the small plane for Alfashir.

The small aircraft flew low altitude ; from it we could see all the land marks of Kordofan and Darfur regions: valleys, mountains, major roads, and some times even towns and moving vehicles. The trip to Alfashir took about three and a half hours.

At Alfashir Airport, I realized after five years' absence how clumsy and rudimental it was and how it remained unchanged since the time of the British. Any thing sweet about it was the fresh air and breath of home sweet home. I call it home because Alfashir had become the dwelling place for my family since the late sixties and early seventies.

Compared to the Nigerian local terminals, Alfashir Airport looked like a mere air strip. There were no taxi cabs or touts like at Nigerian airports. Instead there were only some old trucks and pickups owned by the locals, waiting to be hired. We hired one and left. I was the first to be dropped off at my family house in Hai Elthora, only a few minutes drive from the airport. Adam proceeded to his uncle's where he usually lodged when in Alfashir.

On entering the house, I was received with joy and exaltation by all, especially by my mother and sisters. My father's joy was boundless, and everyone had tears in their eyes except Eshaq, who had been with me in Nigeria only a few months earlier.

Though this was home, I was taken aback by the level of poverty, both of our family and everyone else in the vicinity. Our home was still a mere three huts constructed of wood and straw, a smaller hut for the kitchen, and two structures on the corners used as bathrooms, one for the male members of the family and the other for the females. There was no toilet, only holes in the corners of the bathing structures. Anybody who wanted to answer nature's call had either to use the hole or to wait until nightfall and go to the gorges of the quarry at the outskirts of the town, which was not far from our house.

Although Mother struggled to construct dividing structures within the spacious compound to give privacy to the family from visitors and strangers, it still looked like everybody lived in the same space. In our neighborhood there was not a single house built of brick and mortar or mud. The folks were either laborers or petty traders with a few low-level government workers.

The Wedding

After several days embraced by the warmth of family members, my female relatives decided to see the "*Shaila*" as the tradition demanded. They inspected every item, from *tobes* to dresses, shoes to under garment wears, perfumes to scents and incense. My older sisters selected for themselves some of the best *tobes* which they intended to appear with during the wedding ceremony as tradition demanded.

A day or so afterward, word was sent to the bride's family to be ready to receive me and the Shaila. On the appointed day, there was a lavish party thrown by both families and a bull was slaughtered at the bride's mother's house in accordance with the Zaghawa tradition.

On moving to the bride's house, which traditionally must take place at night, I was barred from entering by the bride's friends. They demanded the traditional "fire lighting" gift. Initially they wanted a large amount of money, but my best man Adam negotiated with them until it was only a token, and then I was allowed to enter and meet the bride.

A week later, Hayat and I left Alfashir for Khartoum, leaving behind family and friends. In Khartoum, I was well received by my friends as well as relatives of Hayat, especially by her older sister, Sadia. A large party was thrown in Omdurman by my cousin Adam Ibrah, the older brother of Rajab, where for the first time both Hayat and I danced and reveled to the lyrics of Jallaba music and America Disco till day break.

A few days later we left for Nigeria. Hayat fell in love with Lagos at first sight. Other parties were also given for us to celebrate our marriage by my colleagues and friends. Thus we settled into our new life together. Hayat was fast to learn the Nigerian local Pidgin English and soon formed friends with the local ladies of Lagos.

Adam Shugar also lived up to his promise and came back to Kano from Sudan with his family. Reunited, our political dreams began to come to fruition.

CHAPTER TEN

*F*ormation of the Salvation Front

Our discussions on forming a political organization which could bring together the people of Darfur and other marginalized forces continued throughout 1986 and part of 1987, but it was kept within our small group. We believed few among Sudanese community in Kano and Lagos supported our cause, not because they were content with the regime or the system, but simply because the majority of the Sudanese in Nigeria in those days, apart from visiting Zaghawa traders, consisted of two categories. They were either Sudanese of Nigerian origin - Hausa and Fallata or riverine Jallaba. The Hausa and Fallata marginalized in Sudan and so they identified themselves with Nigeria as home. The Jallaba were business men and expatriates who consider themselves as part of the ruling stablishment and viewed our endeavor as a Zaghawa project, and part of greater Zaghawa dream for statehood.

This was also the time the rumor of a greater Zaghawa state began to circulate in the region and we believed that the Sudanese intelligence was behind it. Our objective was to create a new political reality in Sudan, even if it meant resorting to armed struggle.

I was a frequent visitor to Shugar in Kano. One thing which made our communication easier in later days was that Shugar got a furnished office with a telephone to run a commission business. The facility helped us to communicate at least twice a week, sometimes daily.

Towards the end of 1986, the differences between the Zaghawa members of GUNT on the policy toward N'Djamena became so deep that they splintered and aligned themselves in two opposing groups. The smaller group was lead by Abas Koti and the other biger group by Adam Togoye. The Koti group distrusted the GUNT leadership, especially concerning finances, and was all for reconciliation with Habré's regime. Togoye's group, which was the *de facto* GUNT, was determined to remove Habré.

These differences had their bearings on our Zaghawa solidarity project. At the beginning of 1987, Abas Koti returned from Libya to Nigeria. He visited me with a Sudanese friend of his from Darfur named Mohammad Mansor Shartaye. I was delighted to see Koti again after more than a year. I discovered his Sudanese friend Shartaye was a member of Democratic Unionist Party in opposition. He was one of the aids of Sharif Hussein al-Hindi, a former finance minister in the second parliamentary regime and a prominent Nemairy opponent in the early seventies, who died in exile and was buried in Baghdad on Saddam Hussein's request.

Koti disclosed his main differences with GUNT and his resolve to reconcile and make peace with Habré's government. Another objective for his reconciliation with Habré was to get inside Chad and pursue the Beri unity from within.

In the following weeks and months, he and his group, which included Mohammad Sabir, opened a dialogue with N'Djamena, culminating in an agreement which stipulated the integration of their fighters into the Chadian army. The agreement also appointed Koti as a diplomat. He was later posted to Sudan as Chargé d'Affaires. Sabir was also appointed to an administrative position.

The departure of Koti and his group from GUNT set the stage for more divisions within GUNT and disagreements between its top leadership and the Libyan authorities. At one point, Gukuni Wedeye, the GUNT leader, was shot at in Tripoli.

Adam Togoye also fell out with Gukuni Wedeye and the Libyan authorities, and at one time he was also targeted for elimination in the GUNT controlled areas of Northern Chad. He withdrew to N'Djamena-controlled areas, where he held secret meetings with government officials and rallied his fighters to the government side. He then departed to France to make a formal statement about GUNT's relations with Libya, and then flew back to the French-speaking countries of West Africa and Nigeria, where he lodged in a posh hotel near the Lagos International Airport and sent for me late one night.

Togoye briefed me on the events in Northern Chad as well as Libya's policy toward his country, with which he disagreed. The objective of Libyan policy as he explained was full control of Chad and its resources, and as long as Libya continued to intervene in the internal affairs of Chad, the country would not see stability or political sanity.

It was clear that he was deeply offended by Libyan policies, this let to seek an opening for further rapport between his group and N'Djamena, and an agreement which would allow him to join the Habré's government.

Events later showed that Habré was not keen in welcoming the politically savvy and over-bearing Togoye back to N'Djamena. In the following weeks and months, Togoye shifted base from Tripoli and Cotonou to Kano, where he also got in touch with Shugar. When I visited them in later months, they were happily engaged socially and in business. They also talked of Zaghawa solidarity more in general terms rather than an immediate objective, while Shugar seemed immersed in the business with Togoye's aids.

Togoye's differences with Libyan authorities and his shift of base from Libya to Nigeria set the stage for the demise of GUNT, as he had been the driving force of the organization.

In June 1987, I learned that Shugar had left Kano for N'Djamena on an undisclosed mission, which was very uncharacteristic of him and unlike our brotherly relationship and sharing with each other the minutest details of our social affairs and political aspirations and hopes. I tried to figure out his motive behind his sudden clandestine departure and made several calls to his office, which by now was shared with Togoye's aids, and to his circle of friends in Kano, but no one had a clue to what prompted him to leave for Chad.

Togoye was not in town at the time and his aids who shared the office and business with Shugar were also upset that he kept them in the dark about his travel plans to N'Djamena.

This was at a time the relations between the Sudanese democratic government of Sadiq al-Mahdi and the Chadian regime of Hissein Habré had reached their lowest point because of the close relations between Sadiq's government and Libyan regime. The media war between the two governments escalated out of control, fueled by the presence of Libyan Islamic legion forces in Darfur's Saqelnam area - a development, if continued unchecked, would put Habré's regime in nippers, considering the presence of elements of GUNT leadership in Libya.

This was when relations were good between Habré and his Zaghawa commanders, after they had liberated the North from Libyan forces supporting GUNT and penetrated deep inside Libya itself and raided an air base at Matan al-Sara. Habré regarded the presence of the Islamic Legion in Darfur as a direct threat to his regime and was prepared to do every thing possible to remove the Legion from Darfur. This resulted in attacks on bases deep inside Sudan and human rights atrocities and abuses against host communities in Darfur.

A few weeks after Shugar's disappearance from Kano, there were rumors within the Sudanese and Chadian communities in Kano and Lagos that Habré was looking for a Sudanese political figure to form an armed opposition front against Khartoum, and that Shugar went to N'Djamena to sound this and to convince the authorities of his ability to fill the role.

I dismissed the rumor, believing if Shugar wanted to get involved in such an important and grave project, he would have either confided or consulted with me before taking any step. I had reservations regarding his military disposition, but whatever his motives were for concealing the purpose of his mission to N'Djamena, I found within myself every justification to seize every opportunity to form an opposition front on behalf of the people of Darfur against Khartoum's ruling elite.

Several weeks passed and he did not return, but a month later I received a package from him through Ali Abdullahi Nossor, a good friend and a counselor at the Chad Embassy in Nigeria. In it was a letter detailing how he had formed a new political front named the Sudan National Salvation Front (SNSF).

Included in the package was a small pamphlet, a typed political manifesto describing, in very militant terms, the injustice which pervaded the political system of Sudan since independence, and that the SNSF was formed to free the people of Sudan from the injustice and find a just and equitable socio-economic system for the country. That SNSF would fight to the best of its ability and resources to put an end to the sectarian rotation of power among the Jallabas in Khartoum. Part of the pamphlet also contained a constitution of the structure of the organization, but was silent on who was involved in the formation and structure of the new front.

Every thing contained in the declaration went along the lines of discussions we had on Sudan politics. Shugar's actions left me with mixed feelings as to whether my political ideas and opinions had created any impression upon him. In the early days of my association with him, he was the academic of lesser propensity towards political discourse, while I was the political advocate.

One feeling told me that he was trying to satisfy his ego without careful consideration of the consequences, while another told me that he was just being secretive initially and would come back to the drawing board again.

The little-publicized Sudan National Salvation Front was the first political front to come into being by Darfuris since the time of the Sony Front, the Red Flame Front, and the Darfur Renaissance Front in the sixties –The later was largely more socio-cultural and developmental than actual political organizations.

It was my view that if this was a genuine effort and Shugar was putting his life on the line and wasn't just out to make a name for himself, then he deserved every support, because the general political situation in the Sudan and the marginalization of the peripheral forces in the country made it imperative to form a political organization capable of representing the aspirations and yearnings of the people of Darfur and the marginalized areas.

The injustice which pervaded our country was colossal and brutal. We felt that no amount of political dialogue and discourse could make the Khartoumists think of inclusive politics towards the marginalized and give way to equitable power sharing. They crafted a strategy of power sharing among themselves, a strategy which takes on several forms of deception to the rest of the Sudanese who are not from the core North or the three main tribes of Northern Sudan - the Ja'aleyeen, the Shaiqiya, and the Danaqila (or the so called Hamdi triangle), plus those who were considered part of their race.

One form of this strategy is the monopoly and rotation of power among their elites in the military and the political establishment. Military coups which overthrew civilian governments were only a smokescreen to hide the fact that their civilian politicians were exercising the monopoly; so were the scenarios of popular uprisings which brought down the military regimes, only to be succeeded by the same civilian elites.

The political party structures in Sudan were designed to produce presidential candidates from among them by virtue of their control of the party and its resources. Their monopoly extended to all sectors of the society with glaring racism. The hardest evidence of racism was in the South, which had recognized all too well the crude and blind racial bigotry and religious and political intolerance of the riverine Northern elites. These elites saw the Negroid groups, especially those of the South, as only good enough to be their servants but not their equals in politics, wealth and culture. They are ready to expend them to the point of genocide than to compromise with them,for power and wealth sharing.

Before Shugar's latest move, we felt the Khartoum elites must be confronted, but confronting them militarily was an enormous task which required huge material and human resources, the backing of at least one or two of the governments in the region, and a super organization which match the Jallaba organization. The South had the advantage of a better geographical environment for a guerilla struggle and almost all of the neighboring countries had a great deal of sympathy toward the Southern cause. In most cases, they were their brother's keeper, both officially and unofficially.

In Darfur, the situation was even more complex and difficult. In Darfur's situation,Khartoum elite can easily set the Darfuris against one an other and depending on Chad's assistance was not enough, as it lacked both the material resources and organizational sophistication which could meaningfully affect things in Khartoum. Moreover, Chad could easily be vulnerable to destabilization by Khartoum, and Habré himself was a product of Khartoum policies.

Sharing the Secret

A few days after the arrival of Shugar's package, I had another new visitor from Sudan via Chad, besides the several other guests already with me. This was Abdalla Hasaballa Domi, a distant cousin. His father,

Hassaball Domi, is a great-grand uncle of Minni Minnawi, who later played a greater role in the Darfur conflict.

I had met Abdalla Domi briefly in Omdurman in early 1982, shortly before my departure to Nigeria and before he departed to Morocco to study law and public administration on scholarship. He was the same generation and Alfashir high school classmate of my younger brother Eshaq. I had not seen or heard of him again until he suddenly appeared at my place in Lagos in May 1987. Abdalla Domi returned to Sudan after his graduation and spent time in Khartoum before he met my friend Abas Koti in Khartoum, who was serving as Chargé d'Affaires in his country's embassy.

Domi decided to come to Chad with the help of Koti and spent several weeks in N'Djamena as his guest. He had also met Shugar there but was not privy to the political project. His main purpose in coming to Lagos was to seek my advice and help to migrate to the Western Europe, the USA, Canada or Australia. He was a very conservative man and neither drank nor smoked. He was a man of few words but deeply religious, prayed five times a day but never shared his religious beliefs with others.

During the time we spent together in my house, we made great efforts to get him into any of these countries but his visa applications were rejected by every embassy we applied to. At one point he was so desperate that we thought of putting him aboard any cargo ship heading for Europe.

We made contact with a shipping company owned by a Nigerian shipping magnet and Muslim community leader named Alhaji Folaweyo. I was acquainted with him through my work at the embassy and at times rendered him invaluable help on issues related to pilgrimage to Mecca, for him and his followers, but as always the case with the wealthy persons in Nigeria, it was hard to get them to return the favor.

The idea was for the shipping company to hire Domi as an employee and put him on a ship heading to Europe, and then when he reached a Eurpean shore city, he would abandon the ship and smuggle himself into any country, but things turned out to be much more difficult than we planed. We had to think of other alternatives.

Though Domi was a very amiable character and we spent many evenings by ourselves, we never discussed the politics of our country on serious note, because each of us had a different idea about the mindset of the other. While I thought his main preoccupation was leaving Africa for Europe, he also thought of me as minding only my work in Nigeria and taking care of the family.

Several weeks after receiving Shugar's document, I shared it with Domi, who read it and sensed an element of seriousness in the project. After that, our discussions centered on it. Domi explained that "before he left Khartoum, there was a lot of agitation and anger within the Darfuri community. Some intellectuals and academics were even calling for armed resistance against the Khartoum government, including Dr. Sharif Harir, a University of Khartoum lecturer who also Domi's close relative. Dr Harir was a man revered for his academic achievements, both at the University of Khartoum where he graduated with first class honors, and abroad where he earned a Doctorate from the Norwegian University.

Domi suggested that he could make a one week trip to N'Djamena to assess the seriousness of the issue, and then return to Lagos. A week passed and Domi did not return. After several weeks I received two letters from him and Shugar. In his letter, Domi explained the SSF endeavor was a real one and that he had radically changed his plans. Instead of migrating to the West, he wanted to be part of the new organization and was ready to fight for justice, equality, and democracy.

I was amazed by this quick and radical change in his plans. In his letter he also disclosed some names which were part of the SSF. Prominent among these was Ishmael Basher, a Libyan-educated lawyer who had been with SPLA for some time in the South Sudan and left it under controversial circumstances to go to Chad. Domi explained that there was no going back in his decision and that he would be heading to Darfur with others to establish the skeleton of the movement.

On the hour of the departure to Darfur to establish bases, a number of young men from the Zaghawa accompanied Domi, including Abderahaman Tortagree, who became the group's military Chief of Staff, while Domi was their political leader. Shugar did not accompany the group to lead them in the field; he remained behind in N'Djamena.

In Nigeria, the rumors and stories from Chad were wild and largely fabricated. They indicated that Shugar left N'Djamena at the head of the group to Bahai; that he had been well-armed by Habré to establish training bases; and very soon he would start operations.

I heard these stories with reservations and mixed feelings. If they were true, it was both terrible and great. We could be on the verge of a historical change, on our way to a rendezvous with either glory or martyrdom. Yet when the hour of the glory or martyrdom approached, fate was not on our side we were found lacking in not necessarily in heroic qualities which were exhibited by the younger Domi and the group which accompanied him to Darfur.

A few months later, Shugar reappeared in Nigeria, accompanied by a young cousin of his. I was puzzled at the turn of events with him;I also felt that our expectations were rather extravagant, many who falsely tried to exaggerate his efforts felt disappointed.

When I learned of his return, I went to Kano and met him, a man now lean in body and low in spirits. He shared what actually transpired in N'Djamena within the few months he was there and what prompted him to return to Nigeria. It was apparent that he was weakened by several problems he faced in N'Djamena, first of which was that those who lured him into going to N'Djamena to form an opposition group did not stand by him with the finances he badly needed to establish a meaningful political organization. They did not connect him with Habré, who held the purse strings and could have helped him at least on personal funds.

Shugar was present in N'djamena at a time Habré was losing trust in his Zaghawa commanders due to what he sensed as their political ambitions, and began to detain some army commanders in the far north of the country. It was a time of political tensions and grudges coming to head; therefore Shugar, too, was a political suspect.

He was non-committal on his future plans for the SNSF, but indicated that he made the effort not to lead but wanted others like me to lead the organization. It was also evident that he apprehended the foreboding nature of the project,if not backed by a regional power, hence declined to move with Domi and the others to Darfur.

Neither of us could foresee what the future held for the SNSF and Darfur, but it was not long before things became worse for everyone.

Toward mid March, I had a visit from a young Chadian opposition member named Asil Manga. Manga did not belong to GUNT where most Chadian Zaghawas in opposition belonged, but instead belonged to a very small group led by Hassan Fadul, half brother of Sidiq Fadul. Manga came from Cotonu with Hassan Fadul, but Fadul preferred to stay away in a hotel. Manga spent the day at my house and later in the evening I suggested to him to arrange a meeting with Fadul and he did. I accompanied Manga to visit Fadul at the hotel.

I found him with rather confused ideas about what he and his group wanted to achieve in Chad, but one thing was clear to him: Habre' must go and GUNT led by Togoye and others should not be a replacement to Habre' regime.Fadul and Manga left for Cotonu the following day.

CHAPTER ELEVEN

$\mathcal{M}$utiny and Rebellion in Chad

On the morning of April 3rd, 1989, as I prepared to leave for work, I had two visitors. One was Asil Manga, the young man who arranged the meeting between me and Hassan Fadul some weeks earlier, and the other was a Chadian gentleman whom I had never met before. Both were dressed in full Hausa or West African Sahil regalia of costly fabric. Their visit, as well as their peculiar outfits, were puzzling to me, because my Chadian guests who travel from Cotonou usually dressed modestly and arrived at my house late in the day. The border crossing from Benin to Nigeria and formalities also took time.

Asil was quick to explain that they came to me early, on the request of Hassan Fadul, because there were serious developments in Chad which concerned us all:

He started "Yesterday morning there was what seemed like an attempted coup in N'Djamena. Both Hassan Jamous, the Chadian army commander general; Idriss Déby his predecessor; and Abas Koti were implicated. They left the capital with their chief lieutenants and bodyguards in open rebellion. The whereabouts and fate of Ibrahim Hitno, the Minister of Interior, and other prominent Zaghawas remained unclear. "He posed and added "But definitely there will be retaliations against them by Habré and his regime," said Asil.

The other man removed the dark sunglasses he wore and added, "When someone demeans and belittles great and courageous men like Hitno, Jamous and Déby, that will be the consequence." He continued:

"D'jamos and Déby are heroes; these are the men who helped Habré to come to power. Now he will see the consequences of his heinous actions."

This news both surprised and shocked me. I asked Asil what could we do on our side under the circumstances. He said it was Hassan Fadul's view that many Zaghawas would flee Chad and across the border to Cameroon and Nigeria, including some army officers, and some would most likely reach my place in Lagos, as well as Shugar's place in Kano and Ali Shomo's place in Maiduguri. We need to be strong and support them"

With these words, they stood, shook my hand, and left, probably returned to Cotonou.

The group which left N'Djamena on the night of April 1st, 1989, was commanded by Jamous and Déby, whose military credentials and charisma were unquestionable and unsurpassed by any of their contemporary Chadian army officers. They were also assisted by Abas Koti, another veteran of FROLINAT and GUNT, plus Dawsa Déby, Adam Koso, Beshar Musa and others.

At the time it was said that they left the capital with only about seventy officers and combat troops. They made it no secret as to their intention and timing of their departure, despite they knew that Habré had in the capital hundreds if not thousands of troops personally loyal to him and commanded by those trusted by him, and that those forces might be put at any time to the task of stopping them or even annihilating them in the process.

One thing was also clear about Jamous and Déby: they counted on the possibility of other troops loyal to them to rally to them from other garrisons in the north and east on their way to the Eastern Chad and join them.

The presidential guards and what was then known as the Republican guards in N'Djamena pursued them. In the process they clashed several times with heavy casualties before they reached the border with Sudan. Despite their few numbers, they were able to ward off attacks by massive number of troops.

While Déby was lucky not to get wounded, his military colleague and the commander general Jamous was not so lucky. According to talk at the time within Zaghawa, Jamous and Déby were attacked by a large government force close to Sudan border. Each was separately controlling and defending a position, but Jamous was wounded and taken prisoner. Déby himself was in a precarious situation at the time and was in no position to render help, but to his surprise, the attacking force withdrew after they got Jamous. Afterward, Déby crossed with the remainder of their troops to Darfur and made contacts with the Sudanese authorities, who welcomed them.

At the time, the news of Jamous' capture was kept secret from the Zaghawa public, especially from the fighters, in an effort to save the morale. For several months stories were pedaled that Jamous was in the field with his troops while Déby traveled between Khartoum and Tripoli.

The Chadian rebel force which crossed to Darfur headed to Dar Zaghawa, specifically to the bases established by Domi in Orshing and Bameshi. Domi's group welcomed them in the usual Beri spirit and hospitality and shared with them their meager resources. This was a larger force which mostly spoke Zaghawa and was commanded by well-known Zaghawa military figures whose appealing was irresistible to the largely simplistic, demoralized, ill-trained and unprovisioned Domi force.

The months which followed saw them completely absorbed and subordinated to the Chadian commanders; their struggle changed to the defense of their Chadian guests against the brutal attacks of Habré's forces which crossed the borders and descended upon them. In the process, Tortagree, the Chief of Staff, was killed along with most of his Sudanese fighters. In a twist of fate, Domi was absent from his troops at the time.

Domi Caught up in a Dictator's Spider Web

While political intrigues and plots developed within Habré's regime by the beginning of 1989, Abdalla Domi and his group did a lot of work in Darfur to promote the cause of the SSF, which had virtually become their creed. Within a year or so they were able to acquire enough camels for their transportation and establish training bases in Southern Dar Zaghawa and Northern Jebel Marra, particularly in Orshing area of Wadi Sayra. In later years, it became the cradle of the beginning of the Darfur revolution.

After establishing the bases in South Wadi Sayra in North Darfur in the form of make-shift or constantly mobile camps for the fighters of the National Salvation Front (SNSF), and with Abderahaman Tortagree as his Chief of Staff, Domi managed to sneak into Alfashir in early 1988 and made several contacts with Zaghawa traders, soliciting their support morally and materially. This was at a time when his group had launched operations and ambushed several government army convoys and the so-called combined units of army and police on patrols. Khartoum started describing the activity of the group as organized armed banditry, or, "Nahab Almosalah."

Domi also wrote several letters to me, and I believe also to Shugar, and sent them with traders who used to come to Maiduguri for Nigerian goods. Only one of those letters reached me. The rest were either destroyed by those entrusted with them out of fear of being found by the security services, or lost due to disregard for their purpose.

In his letter, Domi explained the high morale of his group,which was diverse and appealed for us to help with materials and financial support so that his men would not become demoralized, or forced to become predatory on the local population and commit unruly acts to sustain themselves. Such acts might harm the civil population and the cause. He might also lose credibility before them if no help came from our side.

I sensed how he felt and shared his predicament. Everybody was afraid of the brutality of the Khartoum- controlled army and the police, but I was also constrained, by both lack of resources and the ability to get others to help in the endeavor. Shugar was in a worse situation: he was imprisoned in his own house in Kano by the same problem confronted by Domi in far away Darfur.

Around March 20th, 1989, Domi made arrangements with his close aids to go to Nigeria to brief us on the situation in Darfur and the condition of his men. He handed over the command to his Chief of Staff, Abderahaman Tortagree, and departed from their camp in the bush of Orshing in South Wadi Seyra with two of his aids, Ali Hamid, a Zaghawa, and Mohammad Abakar, a Fur.

They reached the border by night and made their crossing to a village, very close to Tine. They contracted a driver of an old truck to convey them to Heriba, a town about seventy miles from Tine deep inside Chad, which had better transportation facilities to N'Djamena. They departed that same afternoon and arrived Heriba at night, where they met a friend of Domi's whom he knew from his days in N'Djamena. His name was Saqur and he was also the military commander in charge of the Heriba military zone, but was unaware of Domi's activities in Darfur. Domi informed him of his intention to travel to N'Djamena within the next few days and he agreed to help.

Meanwhile, Habré's government was in panic, pursuing the rebels on one front and making frantic efforts to detain all Zaghawa military and non-military personnel who were loyal or would-be loyalists to the rebels on another front.

Saqur himself was totally oblivious to the events in N'Djamena, as communication was not as developed in those days as it is today. He received a communication through the military radio informing him of arrival of a military transport plane to Heriba with a message for him. Saqur informed Domi and his group that they would be traveling by the plane to N'Djamena.

The plane was carrying an army official of Koran extraction with about a dozen other junior officers and men. They informed Saqur that the commander general of the Chad army, General Hassan Jamous, ordered him to report immediately to the headquarters in N'Djamena and that once he finish his meeting with the commander general, he would be returned by the same plane to his command post in Heriba.

He was told to board the plane immediately, not even given the opportunity of informing his family of his departure to N'Djamena and managed only to send the message through aids. Saqur asked Domi and his two aids to join him in the plane, all took off to N'Djamena.

On arrival to the N'Djamena airport, according to Domi he noticed that there was an unusual amount of military presence in the area. As they disembarked, another stern looking senior officer approached Saqur, and after military salutations from Saqur, he demanded that Saqur hand over his service pistol. They were then asked to get into a military vehicle. As the vehicle drove off, Domi told Saqur that he and his companions wanted to get out at a certain location. Saqur relayed the request to the driver but it was ignored.

They arrived at a military base where there was a lot of activity. The vehicle stopped in front of a building where Domi and his group were told in a harsh tone to get out and stay there while the vehicle took Saqur to the inner quarters of the base. They were ordered to a room, where to

Domi's shock and surprise, my friend Ali Abdullahi of the Chad Embassy in Lagos, Nurien Abderahaman, who was also with the Chadian mission in the Republic of Benin, and two others whom Domi did not recognize, were sitting on the floor in handcuffs.

Domi approached Abdullahi and wanted to ask him what was going on, but he was restrained by an armed soldier. They were then interrogated one by one. The questions centered on whether they were Zaghawas, and if so, to which branch and clan they belong, and about their relationship with Jamous and Déby and what did they know about them and their whereabouts.

Domi and his group were handcuffed and taken in a vehicle out of the military base to a large compound, which turned out to be a torture chamber and a prison. They were not allowed to speak to each other, but Domi knew that something was seriously wrong with the Zaghawas in the government.

In the compound they managed to speak to each other. Abdullahi explained in Zaghawa that there were serious problems in the town between the government and the Zaghawa commanders of the army. Consequently, Hassan Jamous, Idriss Déby and Abas Koti and others left N'Djamena in rebellion. The government was now cracking down on Zaghawas in N'Djamena and other places in Chad. Only then Domi and his group understood their precarious situation.

In the prison each was put in a separate cell. The cells were so small that they couldn't stand up straight. For nearly forty eight hours, no food or water was served, neither were they taken out to answer nature's call. On the third day early in the morning, the cells were opened and a hoarse voice ordered all the prisoners to come out and stretch their limbs.

There was a large number of prisoners, including other Zaghawas and many other people from different tribal groups. Domi recognized my old friend Sidiq Fadul, who defected from GUNT some months before and went to N'Djamena, but was incarcerated by the regime simply because he had contacts with his brother Hassan Fadul, who was in the opposition.

Domi also met his friend Saqur and his SSF associate Ishmael Basher. An hour later they were ordered back to their cells. The hoarse voice ordered them to stick out their hands through the openings of the iron bars of their cell doors to get their food. Two prison officials carrying a sack of maize flour passed through the row of cells, filling each hand with the flour. Another two followed with a bucket of water and small metal cups of about sixteen ounces each, filling them with water and handing them to the prisoners. The hoarse voiced declared, "That is your meal for the day!"

It became the routine every two days to be taken out of the cells to stretch their limbs and be given the same amount of flour and water. At times it was dry rice or ungrounded maize. No salt or meaty stuff was ever served.

Domi developed a system to sustain himself with the meager flour and water. He divided the flour to portions for morning and evening meal times. Although it was difficult in the beginning, his body soon adapted to that mode of feeding. Other people could not adapt, especially those who were used to affluence. Their bodies became emaciated, their health deteriorated, and many died.

The morning gatherings allowed them to get acquainted, commiserate with each other, develop a spirit of camaraderie of fellow sufferers, and to know their numbers.

Among those imprisoned were people marked for execution, which was carried out in the middle of the night or the wee hours of the mornings. Although Domi did not literally witness any executions, he and others always heard the dreadful noise made by the executioners at the cell of those taken out for execution. On the mornings when they were taken out to stretch, they would know who was missing amongst their number. A terrible feeling of fear and dread gripped everyone. Some of those marked for execution would simply be starved to death. His friend Saqur was among those.

As the weeks and months passed without any change in their condition, Domi resigned himself to his fate. He was certain that he was going to die, but he also kept praying for God's miracle. At night he had no or little sleep, and when he did sleep, he had terrible nightmares like *Hammer House of Horror*, the British TV series that he used to watch in my house in Lagos. Flashes of those terrible episodes and others from American films were always in his nightmares.

While Domi languished in Habré's prison, whomever remained from his fighters in Darfur became ciphers in terms of the original objective.

CHAPTER TWELVE

$\mathcal{S}$haring the Burden in Lagos

As predicted by Hassan Fadul and Asil Manga, not quite a week from the news of the events in N'Djamena, I had a flurry of fleeing Zaghawa arrivals from Chad, as did Shugar in Kano. These included politicians, businessmen, former government officials, military officers and soldiers.

The very first to arrive to Lagos were Mohammad Salih Adam Jero, a former journalist and businessman, who later became Minster of Interior in Déby's first cabinet, and Adam Badur and Ibrahim Kosi - both prominent N'Djamena businessmen who were closely related and linked to both Hassan Jamos and Abas Koti. Their arrival to Lagos was not to stay but to register with the United Nations High Commission for Refugees, then return to Maiduguri, where they expect more refugees to cross from Chad.

I played host to the three and fulfilled all the required Zaghawa hospitality. Two days later they got their documents from the UNHCR and returned to Maiduguri. Not long afterward, others came with varying purposes. Some wanted to stay briefly and get their documents from the UNHCR and leave, while some wanted to stay longer. Others were officers or soldiers who wanted to proceed to either Libya, from where they would travel across the deseret to the field and join the rebels, or to Sudan through the Central African Republic and then join the rebellion in Darfur. Among them was then Commander Esakha Deyar, a well known prominent fighter and Zaghawa linquist.

In the months which followed, I constantly received and sent off these guests, which continued until Déby took over N'Djamena.

A few months later, my friend Shugar surprised me by coming to Lagos, accompanied by his cousin Mobarak. He declared his intention to travel to Libya to join the rebels in Darfur. Although I advised him against such a move, he insisted. His logic was that among the fighters with Déby in Darfur were those of his former SSF, and that if he appeared in the field, he would be recognized as their leader.

It was an unwise assumption. The one thing he failed to realize at the time was that an army can only have one overall commander; there cannot be two Caesars. This was also at a time which followed a major battle between Habré's forces and the rebels commanded by Déby in Bamishi area of Darfur, where the rebels recorded their first victory, a battle in which also most of Domi's fighters were killed. Yet even with these two different opinions, we remained friends and brothers all the same. He was my honored guest and I his caring host.

Some weeks later Hassan Fadul visited from the Republic of Gabon, where he was met by that country's president Omar Bongo and given some financial assistance. Shugar and Hassan agreed to travel together to Libya,and I wished them lock and regards to Deby and his men.

The two traveled to Libya,August 1989 where they met Déby and Koti. They told Shugar that there was no need for him to proceed to Darfur, so he remained in Tripoli with Koti, who was a liaison between the rebels and the Libyan authorities.

Through out the remainder of the year Habry's forces pressed hard to eliminate the rebellion. The attacks took place inside Darfur in Dar Zaghawa where the local population suffered heavily, either as a result of being specifically targeted by Habry's forces or as a result of being with the cross fire of the opposing forces.

Towrdas the end of June 1989, the democratic regime of Sadik Almahdi was overthrown in a military coup. The leader of the coup, Brigadier Omar Hassan Albashir, declared that he has taken over the power to save the country from economic and political mismanagement of the politicians, as well as put an end to the war in the South, where the Sudan armed forces were experiencing heavy losses and the SPLA was gaining more territories and political recognition internationally.

Brigadier Albashir also declared that his regime will be a nationalist military regime, without political or party affiliation.

As I followed the unfolding of the events in Sudan, I felt a great uncertainty on the situation of the Chadian rebels there. It was clear that Habré could mend his relations with the new regime.

Towards the end of 1989, my guest Adam Badur was attacked by agents of Habré in Lagos while on his way to the Republic of Benin. He was hit by a hit and run car driven by an anonymous person. Luckily for him, he only had a fractured leg. Good Samaritans brought him to me at the Embassy; I rushed him to the Lagos orthopedic hospital, where he his leg was plastered. For the next six months, I nursed him until his leg healed.

While Badur recovered and recuberated in my house, Mohammad Ali Abdallah (Arda sham)- who later became prominent in Déby's rebel movement and subsequently in his government - came from Libya as emissary from Deby. He was accompanied by Shugar's cousin Mobarak Mokhtar. His mission was to provide the resources for the fighters who wanted to go to the field in Darfur through Libya. We provided accommodation and transport for those who wanted to go to Libya. Hundreds of officers and fighters were sent to Libya through the Lagos Airport. Mabarak and Salah Joffon played a major role in this regard.

Towards mid May 1990, almost every would-be fighter who wanted to join forces with the rebels in Darfur had left. It was also time for my annual vacation. I traveled to Sudan to join Hayat and our children, Amal, Ahmed and the newborn Bishara, who had left earlier in December 1989, and also to fulfill my parents' long-time wish of going on pilgrimage to Makkah in Saudi Arabia

I arrived Khartoum via Jeddah as often the case, and few days later departed for Alfashir.

During my stay in Alfashir I met Dawsa Déby and other senior Chadian Zaghawa rebels. Dawsa and others bitterly complained about their discomfort with the Darfur regional authorities.

By mid July I made arrangements for my parents to go on pilgrimage, and they successfully performed their Haj by August 1990. This was also the time my grand mother Hawa Harai passed away to join her ancestors at the age of ninety.

Déby Takes Over in Chad, November 1990

By the time I returned to Lagos in the autumn of 1990, relations between the new military regime in Khartoum and Habré's regime in Chad were mended. It was a U-turn from the hostile relations between the democratic regime of Sadiq al-Mahdi and Habré's, though the new Khartoum junta was still courting Gaddafi, whose hatred for Habré was measurable only to his hatred for Israel and America.

The new junta viewed Déby as Zaghawa assertion and a potential danger to Arab project of total Arabization of the region. He was viewed as obstacle even more than Habré, due to the fact that Déby was a Zaghawa and French trained and oriented and belonged to the same political school of thought of Habré. Khartoum managed to convince Gaddafi that Déby would not be his stooge in N'Djamena and advised to demobilize and disarm him. On this both Tripoli and Khartoum planned to move gradually, as Déby's army was armed to the teeth, strong and battle hardened due to many clashes they had with Habré's forces in Darfur. They feared any precipitated action would lead to heavy casualties.

The Khartoum authorities requested Déby to move his forces to the Nakhila desert oasis, thousands of kilometers away from each of the three capitals, and promised every support would be given to him to train his forces. However, this was a trap to isolate, encircle, and starve Déby's army, and then force him either to surrender or fall pray to Habré's forces.

Déby was an intelligent military officer; he had intelligence reports about the plans being hatched against him. He made a decision which bore similarities in many respects to Bonaparte's decision in 1815 when he escaped from Alba and entered France. Déby had already made up his mind and reached a decision, but he gathered his commanders and explained the situation to them and sought their counsel anyway. The reaction was unanimous. They would only move to Chad and not to any isolated desert oasis.

As always, his fighters' determination was augmented with the reality that there was no going back. It was either absolute victory and glory, or defeat and total annihilation.

On November 24th, 1990, he made his move against N'Djamena. The main body of his forces met with Habré's forces commanded by habre' himself personally at Tine Jagraba in what was described then by some observers as one of the largest battles in modern African history. The two sides were nearly similar in both number of men and armament, but Déby had the tactical superiority.

At the end of a sporadic and grisly battle, Habré lost nearly two thousand and seven hundred men in action, while Déby lost only a few hundred. Habré fled the battlefield in unmarked regular military vehicle and radioed N'Djamena from Omshaloba to be airlifted. The rest of his commanders who survived either captured or willingly rallied to Déby's side.

The battle of Tine Jagraba was a decisive victory to Déby and marked the end of Habré's era. The rest of the way to N'Djamena was a nearly unopposed military march.

As the events at the Chad border started unfolding against the Khartoum's and Tripoli's wishes, Khartoum was angered and moved against the prominent Zaghawas in Darfur and threw them in jails, then sealed off any possible retreat routes for Déby and his forces. When Déby entered N'Djamena victorious, the detainees were released in cluding Domi and his colleagues.

At the same time, another war of a different nature was initiated against the Zaghawas in Darfur, especially in South eastern and Central Darfur. Under the pretext of countering armed banditry, Sudan government military, police and other security forces targeted Zaghawa villages and Zaghawas in the localities of Shearia, Khazan Jedid, Wadaa, Mahjeria, Lebedo and Khor Abeche in Eastern and Central Darfur. Zaghawas were also targeted in South Darfur in the administrative localities of Aldaain, Buram and Hofrat En Nahas.

The attacks on the villages bore similarities to the attacks which occurred during the genocide. Zaghawa villages were burned to the ground and promenet members of Zaghawa communities were rounded up and executed.

One such incident occurred in Shearia in March 1991. A combined force of military and police in three trucks arrived in Shearia at midnight and went to a Zaghawa area of the town and rounded up all men from their homes. At the police station, their names were taken, then eight of the prominent members of the community were selected and loaded into vehicles while the rest, including their family members, were told to leave.

Among the eight who were taken were my uncles,the brothers Mahmoud Senin and Bakhit Senin.

The force immediately left Shearia with the detainees. They gave the impression to the families of the detainees that they would be taken to the force state head quarters in Neyala. After driving forty miles from Shearia, the force diverted to a bush below a hill known as Debelkora. They brought down the eight Zaghawas, who were in chains, and shot them in cold blood, buried them in a mass grave.

The family members of the executed went to Neyala to find them, but there was no trace of them and the security forces were not forthcoming as to their where abouts. A search party was set up from the families and the rest of the Zaghawa community in Shearia. After several days the mass grave was discovered and the bodies exhumed. A Zaghawa medical doctor Ibrahim Mahmoud Imam played a major role in the identification and reasons for the death.

This incident infuriated the Zaghawa population in Shearia and throughout Darfur. The families petitioned the government to the highest level, but nothing was done. There was no investigation and no detention of the officers who led the force to Shearia that fateful night.

One of the prominent petitioners was Dr. Sharif Harir, the Khartoum University lecturer and a close relative to both Bakhit and Mahmoud Senin. He earlier had a bad experience with these forces when they attacked another Zaghawa village in the vicinity of Alfashir where he was visiting relatives. He was able to intervene and save the villagers that day, putting his life on the line by appealing in Khartoum Arabic to the commanding officer.

Harir petitioned the head of state with Nor Ali Hassan, the family head of Bakhit and Mahmoud and the other relatives of the victims, but because of his petition, he was subjected to the scrutiny of the dreaded state security service, the SSS. He became a man of interest to these forces and was warned by a Darfuri close friend of his in the government of the fact, who also advised him to flee the country. Luckily for him, he had his family in Norway,and could travel there.

The Formation of the DSJE, July 1992

By December 1991, I had made several trips to N'Djamena, partly to see the progress made in pacification and governance by Déby's MPS and partly as a personal effort to bring together some of the young men from Sudan side of the border who fought with Déby to N'Djamena. I also investigated whether it was possible to reconstitute the SSF or instead create an alternative political organization and map-out strategy. I planned to approach my old friend Abas Koti and through him, Déby, for support and assistance in our struggle, even if it meant political support only.

It had never occurred to me nor to our people who fought with Déby to N'Djamena that it would be politically naïve and inexpedient to seek such support at that particular time from the politically pragmatic Déby, who wanted to maintain cordial relations with Khartoum by all means. It was clear that he had adopted the principle of the *end justifies the means*, which in politics means that there are no permanent friends or enemies.

Whatever understanding was reached, at the time Déby was in the bush, on giving support to the SSF was subjected to this political expediency. The Sudanese Zaghawa fighters in his army were treated as Chadian soldiers and a policy of their dispersal to remote areas of Chad was pursued. Apart from Koti, who became popular within Zaghawas of Sudan on account of the good relations he established while serving in Chad Embassy, Déby's other Zaghawa officials spoke only on the pacification of Chad and consolidation of MPS regime, and when they spoke of Beri unity, they spoke in these terms.

Koti became busy with the position of the Commander General of the Chad National Army and later Minister of Defense. I had difficulty meeting him due to his busy schedule, and when I finally succeeded, he had little time to discuss the issues, even though he faintly reiterated his earlier position on the issue.

On my trips to N'Djamena, I had several clandestine night meetings with a select group in a back room in Adam Burma's house. The young men who attended these meetings were energetic and enthusiastic chaps who only needed good guidance and some resources to swing into action, but what could have been very positive and good outcome of those meetings were frustrated and watered down by silly personal differences and clan bigotries - the problem even today with the Darfur armed opposition against Khartoum. Everyone in our N'Djamena meetings wanted to be the head of whatever organization was agreed upon, or wanted someone from his clan to be the head.

The key personalities in N'Djamena efforts were Abdalla Domi and Ishmael Basher, veterans of the Salvation Front. Though former colleagues and comrades and fellow sufferers of Habré's brutality, the problem largely emanated from their rancorous relationship.

From the start, Ishmael took everyone for granted and assumed the role of a leader, volunteering or forcing himself to chair the meetings, a thing detested by Domi, who knew him better than anyone among us and who also did not forget the earlier lackluster role played by Ishmael when he refused to go with the SSF group to Darfur, leaving Domi and the rest to face the danger.

At our last meeting, things were so bad between the two that any proposal advanced by one of them was met by a counter proposal from the other or someone supporting him. While Ishmael wanted to play the role of the big brother who knew all and must lead, Domi, besides the feeling of betrayal, had also his own misgivings regarding Ishmael's fitness to lead.

At one point Domi interjected the issue of Ishmael's health. While Ishmael denied that he had any health problem, it was Domi's view that he suffered from a serious illness, probably tuberculosis, and he could not lead. Ishmael flew into a rage and accused Domi of scheming to become the leader himself. Whether Domi raised the issue as a political maneuver or gimmick, or if the man was genuinely ill, was hard to tell at that moment, but events since showed that all was not well with Ishmael's health, as he died a few years later from a mysterious illness.

I restrained myself, trying to play the roles of the wise man and compromiser, pleading with them to bury personal ambition for the sake of our noble cause, but to no avail. In the early hours of a March 1991 morning, our meeting ended without a resolution, and everyone departed the place in funeral silence.

Though I had very little sleep the previous night, I had to leave for Nigeria later that morning. Domi escorted me to Kousseri on the Cameroon side of the border through the river crossing, which was a short distance from Burma's house.

At the crossing point we met the officials in charge busy with some new comers with heavy load from the Cameroon side, and were paying little attention to those crossing to the other side. They were more concerned on the commission or fee they could collect from those coming in to the country, than watch who was crossing and who was not. Domi indicated that we could make the crossing without alerting them, and we did.

As we breakfasted in Kousseri, we reflected on the previous night's meeting. Despite the difficulties of forming a political organization, we knew we must carry on with the struggle by all means. Domi wanted to get back to Darfur as soon as possible to study the situation and the possibility of reestablishing his old training camps in South Wadi Sayra. I pointed out that he needed resources, but he said that all he needed was the cost of road transportation from N'Djamena to Darfur and back again to N'Djamena, which was about one hundred thousands African Francs, or about two hundred US dollars by then. It was an amount I could afford to give and could still make the journey to Lagos.

A few weeks later, my cousin Abdeljabar Abakar, who had recently finished his studies in Libya and graduated with BA in political science, came for a visit, along with Ishmael Hashim, another cousin who earlier had traveled with me to N'Djamena when Déby took over power in November 1990.

Abdeljabar was a young graduate in the wilderness, and just like Domi some four years before, he came to Nigeria seeking solutions to many problems: political, educational, and employment. I had long discussions with both of them about the situation in the Sudan, and despite their age, they exhibited a degree of political understanding which earned my admiration.

I explained to Abdeljabar how I traveled to N'Djamena in an effort to establish a political organization which worked to champion the rights of the marginalized people, and how Domi was a selfless man in the cause, and that his journey to Darfur was an important effort in line with his earlier efforts of 1987 to 1988.

Abdeljabar was enthusiastic, a blend of Zaghawa manhood and a student of political science, fostered by Libyan Jamahiriya revolutionism. He was more than willing and eager to subscribe to any political project which could change the situation in Sudan.

Several months later, Domi returned from Darfur to N'Djamena and we agreed that Abdeljabar should go to Chad with funds to enable him to reach us in Lagos. Abdeljabar traveled around October 1991 and a week later he, Domi and Khatir Arko, a veteran of Sudan's army who joined Déby's army in 1989, came back.

It was a great gathering. Domi reported that the situation in Darfur was going from bad to worse. The new regime which took over in June 1988 had already initiated what looked like an ethnic cleansing policy, directed mainly against the Fur and the Zaghawa. The Governor of Darfur, Altyb Saikha, ordered the containment of Zaghawa in a large concentration-like cluster of villages in South Darfur. Any Zaghawa found out side of this cluster was treated as a criminal and dealt with as such, including execution. There was also what looked like genocide against the Fur in Jebel Marra and Wadi Salih by Arab groups armed by the government.

Upon hearing this news, we reflected on the events of March 1991, when my uncles Mahmoud Senin and Bakhit Senin and six others were executed by government security forces, the thing which made Dr. Sharif Harir petition the government, and eventually flee the country. We thought of him as possible leadership material that our movement would benefit from his knowledge and expertise.

As we weighed him against other personalities, some one suggested that Harir could be the leader we are looking for,he could be the champion for the cause of the marginalized in a country dominated by an ethnic elite who ran the affairs of the country in a quasi-Colonial style.

We decided to invite him to Lagos for an urgent meeting which would culminate in the formation of a political organization to replace or supersede the Sudan Salvation Front. This new organization would represent us in the struggle against the policies of Khartoum and present our cause to the rest of like-minded Darfuris and the marginalized in opposition.

Around mid-November 1991, Domi, Ismael Hashim, Abdeljabar Abakar, Khatir Arko, and myself went to the Nigerian Central Telephone Exchange, known as NITEL, the only medium for international calls by then, to call Dr. Harir. We reached a man in high spirits and ready to take part in any endeavor which would bring change in Sudan. He agreed to come down to Lagos to meet our group. We did not have resources to cover his tickets, but he assured us that he could take care of the issue. Some public-spirited Zaghawas were ready to donate funds, and by that he would come with whatever was raised. I worked through my contacts at the Nigerian ministry of foreign affairs especially through my friend Ambassador Saka Fagbo, to get him the visa to Nigeria.

A few weeks later he flew in to Lagos Murtalla Mohammad International Airport. The following day we wasted no time and immediately discussed the situation in Sudan as reported by Domi. Harir also briefed us on his activities since he left Khartoum. He was in contact with Ahmed Diraige in London and had an understanding with him on the urgent need to form a political organization which could represent, "the lost voice." Dr. Harir also presented a paper on his vision regarding the political future of the Sudan. We unanimously adopted it as our political declaration.

We spent whole nights in discussions on the situation in Sudan and how to frame the constitution of a new political organization. We also pondered the fate of the SSF and the whereabouts of Shugar, whom we learned was in Kano at the time. We assigned the task of drafting the constitution to Domi and Harir, which they did well. It would guide our new political organization, which we named the Democratic Solidarity for Justice and Equality - DSJE. We also unanimously assigned the responsibility of the Secretary General to Dr. Harir, to be deputized by Bahar Arabie.

To affirm that the formation of the organization was a continuation of a political process started some five years earlier, we prepared a carefully worded letter to Shugar, informing him of the formation of the DSJE, not as a replacement of the SSF, but as evolution of it, and that the membership of the new organization was open to all adult Sudanese, regardless of their sex, ethnic belonging, creed or religious belief. It also stated that the DSJE would fight to achieve the aspirations and objectives of the marginalized in Darfur and throughout Sudan.

No press conference or formal declaration through the media was made because at the time we had our own security concerns, as the Khartoum government also brought to Nigeria an NIF fundamentalist as ambassador and it was easy in 1992 to hire assassins in Lagos to eliminate an opponent. It was not uncommon to see mutilated dead bodies of people by the waysides of major streets of Lagos, such as Lagos-Ibadan Expressway, Ikorodo Express, and Mile 2 Express. Elimination could take several forms or scenarios: armed robbery, kidnapping and killing in way which looked like car accident, or handing over to the opponent.

The few days which followed the formation of the DSJE, we were euphoric and had high hopes. We felt a sense of achievement, but we also apprehended the dangers and the enormous task ahead of us. We viewed it with a sense of responsibility, especially since this was a time when the war in the South Sudan was intense and the Nigerian government was venturing to mediate between the Sudan government and the SPLA.

A few days later, Dr. Harir left for Norway via London, where he stopped and briefed Diraige on the formation of the DSJE. Diraige had his own political organization which had Federalism as an objective, and he wrote extensively on the issue of suitability of a federal system in Sudan. Diraige's reaction was positive and proposed and alliance between his group and the DSJE. We felt delighted that Diraige, with all the political experience and his resources, would be part of the project and looked ahead to his leadership and to a bright future for the movement.

The letter about the DSJE to Shugar was carried by Domi, his old political associate in the SSF. He met him in Kano and briefed him on the formation of the DSJE. Shugar did not object or comment, and from all indication it seemed that he had resigned to the fact that the SSF had become history.

After meeting with Shugar in Kano, Domi proceeded to Chad to work to advocate and recruit members for the DSJE from within the Sudan Zaghawa in Chad and others Sudanese who accepted the goals and objectives of the movement. Several weeks later he was joined by Khatir, while Abdeljabar and Ismael Hashim remained with me in Lagos. The news of the formation of the DSJE traveled fast and reached the Zaghawa community, especially the Sudan Zaghawa community in Chad, even before the arrival of Domi and Khatir.

In N'Djamena they were faced with a difficult environment due to the ubiquitousness of Sudanese intelligence agents, even from fellow Zaghawas, and they worked under the strictest secrecy, only trusting people within the former SSF.

In Chad, the political honeymoon between the men who fought to overthrow Habré and establish a new and just political system was over. Differences and mistrust appeared between president Déby and his former army chief and Minister of Defense, who was later relegated to the lesser position of Minister of Public Works.

These differences centered on control of power and wealth, so instead of collaborators, they became rivals. At the end of the day, the president had the upper hand and control of the situation. Koti and his followers left Chad to start a new rebellion. I followed the unfolding of these events with pain because they forebode the ruin of the Zaghawa solidarity which we worked to achieve since 1983.

As a result of these developments, the situation within Zaghawa community in N'Djamena grew complicated. There was division between the Chad Zaghawas, either for or against the government. The Wegi section of the Sudan found itself in very difficult situation because of the divide within the family, and under the circumstances it was logical to align with the government, despite Koti's Kobe section's labeling of the Wegi as, "servants of the Bedyat."

We deferred any serious attempts of recruitment within Chad lest it be viewed as supporting Koti's cause. Chadian groups which supported Koti also withdrew to Darfur, where they had clashes with the Sudanese forces. Many of them were killed or captured, though a few managed to establish some bases. Koti crossed to Cameroon with some supporters, where he made scathing attacks against Déby's regime to the international media. They were detained by the authorities but later managed to escape and headed to Libya, then Egypt and Saudi Arabia.

I expected Koti to contact me while in Cameroon but he did not. However, the newly posted Zaghawa officials in the Chad Embassy in Lagos suspected Koti might have contacted me or even reached me in Lagos. They made frantic efforts to find out whether I was hiding some one from his group by visiting my house at odd hours.

Koti's opposition to Déby was both a consequence of bad advice from those around him, a serious miscalculation on his part as to Déby's control of the military, and the support of the neighboring countries and France to his government, specifically Sudan and Libya. Had he reflected on the initial events which led to the success of MPS in 1989 to 1990 and compared them to his circumstances, he would have acted otherwise.

Déby himself acted precipitously. He quickly removed Koti's die-hard supporters within the capital from positions of influence, as well as placated the would-be supporters. Next, he made certain that Koti would not get support from any of the vital countries in the region.

Koti's endeavor was a failure. Exactly a year after his defection, he was already weary and battle-fatigued. His military and political supporters were in disarray. In the end, he was persuaded into accepting peace and returned to N'Djamena in the Autumn of 1993, only to be accused of plotting a coup and killed a few months later by troops loyal to Déby under mysterious circumstances.

CHAPTER THIRTEEN

The Formation of the SFDA

By early 1994, more than two years had passed since the formation of the DSJE, but we achieved little progress due to the situation within Zaghawa.

All this time we kept badgering Harir on how far he had gotten with Deraige on the issue of formation of a united front and securing logistics to mobilize us. If we failed to make headway within Zaghawas, we could hardly win anybody else. We especially wanted to win the Fur for the cause, but Harir's reply was always, "He had done his part," meaning he had asked the supposedly resourceful Deraige to make a declaration and now the matter was with him and there would be progress soon. Little did we know that they were in no better conditions than us.

All this time concerned youths, who were ready to act, were on the move between N'Djamena and my house in Lagos. Domi's dedication for the cause was exemplary. I have to mention here, too, the infatigable efforts of Abas Mohammad Eshaq (Abas Omda), the son of the Omda of a section of Eladegain clan, who also excelled in this endeavor.

By June 1994, we had reached a level of frustration which was best could be described as total despair and anger directed at what we perceived as inability or inaction by men we thought had the resources,capacity and the political wherewithal to lead us and effect the change on the political scene for Darfur itself.

Like most followers of African style leadership, we were oblivious of the constraints they faced, especially by Harir, such as his lack of resources and the refusal of the Zaghawa businessmen he contacted to help in the cause.

We managed to make at least a call every month to Harir and through him to Deraige and others for a bigger political organization.

Sharif's willingness and dedication to the cause was exemplary, but his efforts were countered by Diraige's political calculations, which we perceived - wrongly or rightly - as canniness and hesitation bordering on mistrust of the Lagos group, or of those behind the cause.

In June 1994, Diraige finally agreed to formally declare the birth of the Sudan Federal Democratic Alliance - a merger between his Sudan Federal Organization and our DSJE – in a press conference from London. The initial leadership committee comprised of him as chairman, with Sharif Harir, Suliman Rahal, Abakar Abulbashar and Musa Rahal as members. All except Harir were residents in London and no mention was made of others members outside United Kingdom.

None of them alerted us to the timing of the declaration. We caught up with the news through the BBC *Focus on Africa* program by sheer accident and immediately called to congratulate them and showed our solidarity and support. The English text manifesto, which was described at the time by one Sudanese observer as written in, "a superb English," was Sharif's work with input from all of us. The Arabic text produced by Deraige bore little resemblance to the English version. It was a kind of a political open letter addressed to the general Sudanese public rather than addressing the specifics of the cause. Nevertheless, we felt relieved, and a sense of achievement pervaded our activities. It aleast Deraige

Domi's Disappearance and the Long Wait

Immediately after the declaration, Dr. Harir swung in to action, utilizing all his social and political resources. He believed he could use his old relationship with Déby to persuade him to help our cause; more especially because Déby was a former class mate of his in the late fifties and early sixties. They studied together as young children in Kornoye school of Dar Zaghawa, when Déby's family was refugees in Darfur. He expressed willingness on occasions to visit N'Djamena to seek the president's help, but we cautioned him.

Though both Domi and myself advised Harir against visiting N'Djamena to seek help from President Déby, because of his close relations with Albashir, he went ahead any with his plans and arrived in N'Djamena in October 1994 and lodged with Dawsa Déby, the president's elder brother. His disregard or over rule to our advice was the second ovious sign of lordism in Harir. He asked to see the president but was kept waiting for a long period of time. Later we learned the president had left the country for long vacation abroad which involved a medical checkup, without leaving word for Harir.

Dr. Harir spent close to three weeks in N'Djamena on Dawsa's Chadian-style hospitality, which was becoming a ploy to undermine his dignity. Instead of being treated as a high profile personality with a noble cause, he was turned into someone who could be ignored. He later came down to Lagos from N'Djamena to consult with us.

Most of the senior members of the SFDA in the region were present in Lagos and we held several meetings to map out a strategy. We agreed to keep low profile until the time was ripe, as we knew the regime's agents were every where.

Dr. Harir spent close to three weeks with us before departing to Norway. Our main concern was how to secure finances to advance the objectives of the movement,and to begin action from Darfur. Harir, though a man of academics who resigned his teaching job at Bergen University to devote his time for the cause, was in no better financial situation than us to offer any help. He had only the credential, the will, and persuasive argument to convince potential would be financiers.

A few weeks after Harir's departure, I held a meeting with Domi and Ibrahim Birka, one of the new members of the SFDA. We concluded that instead of waiting for Deraige and Harir to look for finances, that we should also do our part,and create our own resources. While I offered what little savings I had from my work with the Saudis as start-up capital for an investment, Domi and Birka expressed willingness to manage the investment. It was agreed that the two would start an export business between Nigeria and Zaire, in the form of exporting assorted goods from Lagos to Kinshasa. The profits would be used to finance our activities. Towards the end of June the two left for DR Congo with merchandise.

Family Reunion

Meanwhile, in July 1995, my brother Eshaq did another great service to me by bringing my wife and children to Nigeria, who had been away from me in Darfur for over a year. He brought them with my sisters Aisha and Nora, who were on their annual leave from their teaching jobs. They made the arduous journey by road on trucks from Darfur across Chad and Cameroon, a distance of no less than four thousand miles.

I spent long nights conversing with my sisters, especially with Aisha whom I had not seen in over four years. After three months together in Lagos, their holidays were nearing the end and they wished to return to their jobs. I wanted Nora to stay behind with me even if it meant applying for a leave without pay, which she agreed to and sent her application to Sudan.

Aisha and Eshaq returned to Sudan with my two children, Amal, who was nine years of age, and Ahmed, who was seven. She insisted on taking them back because she wanted to do me a service by educating them in her own school and by bringing them up in the Sudanese culture. Their mother and I had misgivings initially regarding their separation from us, but we reassured ourselves since they were going to be within the larger family of grand mothers and grand fathers, aunts and uncles, cousins and other relatives, they would be all right.

I spent the remainder of that year trying to coordinate our political work in West Africa. This was also when the Sudan government intensified its intelligence work in the region, specifically in Chad and Nigeria, all in an effort to monitor our activities.

Sudanese intelligence recruited local agents from among the Sudanese community in Nigeria to spy on us, some of which were my close associates. My house was subjected to all kinds of monitoring and surveilance, from both the locally recruited and from others Sudanese who claimed to be former army or police officers terminated by the NIF regime for what was termed as (public good)but in fact were agents in disgise spying for the regime. At work I felt the loss of the sympathy and understanding of my good friend, Ambassador Alyahya.

Politically, Deraige and Harir did not render much help throughout that year, both in terms of financial and moral support. Despite the good communication facilities at their disposal in London and Oslo, there was a near breakdown of communication. For the time I thought may be they wanted to deal with eiltes rather the commoners like us.

I was becoming the prisoner of circumstance. I longed for every opportunity to set myself free to carry out diplomatic contacts in Nigeria, to make the international community aware of the atrocities going on in Darfur, and to do intensive organizational work, but all these needed resources and a lot of tactfulness in the face of danger posed by the government intelligence agents.

Abdalla Domi and Ibrahim Berka, in whom I had built much hope on their comercial work, were nowhere to be seen or heard of. The absence of any news about them and doubts about their safety troubled me more than what they could or could not achieve.

In early May 1996, I received calls from Eshaq and other relatives and friends about my father's death in Alfashir. Our entire family was deeply grieved. I was particularly saddened because my father died while I was away from him, for I knew he always wanted me to be at his bedside in the event of his death. Both Nora and Hayat wept, and in the absence of other relatives I consoled them. I wished if I could travel to Alfashir to see our mother and our siblings, but it was not possible due to the political problem I faced in Sudan.

Around December 1996, about six months after my father's death, I was approached by Ali Shomo, an old Zaghawa friend who traded and resided in Maiduguri, through other friends (in accordance to Zaghawa tradition), who asked me for the hand of my sister Nora for marriage, as now I stood in the shoes of my father.

Nora was particularly close to me simply because she loved me and wished all her life to be close to me. She left her teaching in Alfashir and Mother and the rest of our siblings to stay with me in Nigeria. Though I had my own misgivings about the suitability of Ali Shomo, because he was already married and had many children with his wife, I presented the issue to my sister but she had no objections. I made the necessary arrangements with Hayat for the ceremony, and with the few Sudanese friends we had, the marriage rites were concluded. Nora left to be with her husband in Maiduguri.

For several months, both Hayat and I and the children felt her absence, but received good news about her. She was expecting a baby, so I decided to visit her close to her thirty-seventh birthday, and also get the latest news about the situation in Darfur.

I arrived in Maiduguri around July 14th and lodged with my sister. Though she looked in good health and her living condition looked relatively comfortable in every respect, she was in low spirits and spoke of her loneliness and longing to see her mother in far away Alfashir. It was particularly troubling that she expressed a desire to sell whatever valuables she had and offer them as charity gifts to the poor, or send them to her mother. It pained me to hear her speak in such a manner, so I decided to spend more time with her.

A week or so after my arrival to Maiduguri, Minni Minnawi - by then Suliman Arko Minnawi - a young man and a cousin, and a younger brother of Khatir Arko who was part of our group that founded the DSJE also came to Maiduguri from Darfur via Chad, and we lodged together at Nora's place. I was delighted at his coming not only because he was a relative, but he also had lots of information about the situation in Darfur. Minni's declared mission to Nigeria or Maiduguri was to pursue an English language course, but from all indications he was also in pursuit of unrevealed higher goals and ambitions. He must have been keenly following our political activities in the DSJE and SFDA and wanted to be part of it. We found an English teaching institute for Minni and he started the course in earnest.

In the weeks which followed, we gave Nora good company. We talked all night about delightful nothings and told our own traditional folk stories in an effort to lift her spirits and she seemed to improve. I was also amazed by Minni's endurance of the Maiduguri mosquito bites, as he often refused to sleep at night inside the mosquito net provided by Nora.

Two weeks later, Nora complained of pains all over her body, so along with her husband, we took her to the best hospital in town, the University of Maiduguri teaching hospital.

The following day she seemed quite normal and did not complain much, but toward evening she told me that she would die soon. I did not take her seriously, as the doctors assured me earlier that day that there was nothing alarming about her condition. She asked me to be closer to her and to hold her head in my hands. I did but her head was so feeble, I grew alarmed and rushed to call a doctor. He seemed shocked and called for other doctors and nurses and they moved her to intensive care. They fought to save her but she passed away. No one could explain why she died.

I wept as I never wept before as I held her body. When I finally left the room to face her shocked husband and Minni, neither could do anything to console me. I was bereft of a loving sister in a country where few knew me and nobody cared. I thought of her mother, brothers and sisters and how would they receive the news of the death of their beloved daughter and sister. It had been not been a long time since some one so dear had died in our family,as my father died the previous year but he was 88 years old. I prayed from my heart for God to give her the eternal perfect peace that she deserved.

In the few hours that followed, we carried her body to her house. Some elderly ladies prepared her body for burial in the Islamic tradition which stipulates the dead should be interned as soon as possible. We buried her that same night.

When we returned from the cemetery, it was after midnight. It was the saddest night of my life. I stayed awake all night, lying on my face in the wide yard in front of her rooms, praying for her soul to be granted entrance to Paradise. As I prayed, I remembered our journey together since childhood and felt that I did not do enough to help her in life. I began to think wild, I could have taken her to Lagos the moment I learned that she was pregnant and afforded her a better healthcare facility. I felt guilty that I gave her away in marriage in a strange country, away from her mother and brothers and sisters.

The closest person in those difficult hours was Minni. Though young in age, he was as gentle and consoling as an elder.

The next morning we were visited by her husband and some of her neighbors, and it was decided that three days later we would hold the traditional general prayer for her. As communications were bad those days, there was no way to communicate the news either to the family in Alfashir or to Hayat in Lagos. I waited the three days in Nora's house together with Minni. At the appointed day of the prayer, there were hundreds of people in attendance; many of these were her neighbors. The holy Quran was recited several times for her departed soul.

Immediately after the prayer I left for Lagos, leaving Minni behind.

When I got home, Hayat could read my feelings even before I broke the news to her. She anxiously asked whether everything was okay, and when I broke the news to her, she cried uncontrollably along with my children.

Hayat was in an even deeper state of mourning than me, as she used to be close to Nora. Under the circumstances, we agreed that, although she was pregnant for few months, should leave with the children-Bishara, Aisha and Abdelhafiz, to Sudan to console the family.

After Hayat's departure with the children, I remained alone for several weeks, my family photo album the only companion to connect me with the rest of my folk. I spent longer periods on Nora's pictures, especially the pictures when she was younger.

Several weeks later, Minni joined me in Lagos from Maiduguri. I found him a great help in my solitude, and soon other friends and members of our political organization joined us from Chad. I also started going out for my small private transportation business which I started after I left my job at the Saudi Embassy, which helped us a lot in our daily living.

Minni also brought with him some very interesting and important recordings of Zaghawa songs. Their lyrics mostly centered on war and the glorification of bravery, and we spent our leisure time enjoying the panegyrics of the legendary vocalist Sharif Karima and the beauty of his vocal variety. They were the kind of songs which could be a sort of martial music to any fighting Zaghawa group.

I believe those songs greatly helped in Minni's motivation, transforming him from a mere high school graduate seeking to improve his English for a better teaching job in Sudan, into a militant military man and a politician in his own right. Those songs also helped rekindle the fighting spirit in many other Zaghawa youth who were to become part of the SLA.

A few weeks from Mini's arrival we were also joined by my cousin and former West Africa magazine correspondence turned free lance journalist Trayo Ahmed Ali, better known in later days as Ali Trayo. Trayo was coming from Chad and heading to Ghana where he was based. We spent great time together reflecting on our politically miserable situation. Mini was of the opinion that "the matter of the revolution does not need resources, just will and raw courage" he went on to say "if Dr Sharif or any a true leader appears in Darfur today the young people will rally around him and protect him". I liked his idea and began some enlightening work with him. Later in the year we were also visited by his elder brother Khatir Arko. I was delighted at his visit. After several weeks I agreed with Khatir that he should head to Darfur on exploratory visit. We gave him whatever we could afford to travel to Darfur and he left. Several weeks later I travelled to Maiduguri on business also to enquire about him,only to find out that Khatir did not leave Nigeria to Darfur but in Maiduguri itself and to my surprise married. When I met him he gave me an acceptable excuse which was,that he learned he was sought after by both the Sudanese and Chadian intelligence therefore he could not cross in to Chad to go to Darfur. I wished him luck in his new life. When I returned to Lagos I told Mini about my agreement with Khatir and how Khatir could not do it. Mini seemed visibly upset with his elder brother's action,but did not elaborate.

By mid 1998, news began to filter in about the where abouts of Domi and Birka. I received a letter from Birka detailing how differences developed between the two on the strategy at the initial stages of the business. Domi left him in Kinshasa and departed for Angolan border to venture in to the diamond trade business. After that, the two lost contact.

In August 1998 Domi appeared in Zaire in a rather bad financial situation and travelled to Birka in North Zaire. His own account was that he was arrested at the Angolan diamond fields by the Angolan rebels of Jonas Savimbi in late 1994. Whatever he had was confiscated and thereafter he spent the next four years in their custody in conditions very similar to Habré's prison in N'Djamena, only to be released after the death of the UNITA leader.

Whatever business venture there, was completely lost, but the two managed to get together, mend their differences and start anew in North Zaire,but this time around just between the two of them. They also agreed to refund the capital money I provided,but again they parted ways. After the flaring up of the revolution in Darfur, Domi headed for Darfur to be part of the the revolution and an important figure in the movement until his assassination, while Birka migrated to the USA.

CHAPTER FOURTEEN

$\mathcal{B}$etween Maiduguri and Abuja

It was never my intention to settle in Maiduguri in Borno State of Nigeria, the spot (traditionally called Yerwa) from where Mahamat Bornawe migrated to Beri Beh or Dar Zaghawa of today, and where my dear sister Nora is buried. I wanted to maintain a link with the commercial town, because as I mentioned else where in this book, it had become an important source of profitable goods for Zaghawa traders from Sudan.

Scores of Zaghawa traders frequented Maiduguri since our early days in Kano with Shugar, and I thought it would be good to maintain contacts with those coming from Darfur to remain up-to-date on the situation on the ground. I started going to Maiduguri at least once every month, taking with me sellable commodities to finance my trips and also to send to my family in Darfur.

By October 1999, Hayat and the children had been away from me for eighteen months and I was eager to see them. However, I was not in a position to travel to Darfur and had no means to bring them to Nigeria.

At the beginning of November 1999, I received a pleasant surprise. My brother Eshaq telephoned me from Maiduguri and informed that he was in Maiduguri with Hayat and two of my children, Abdelhafiz and Nora-named in memory of her aunt. It was such joyful news that I left Lagos immediately by commuter bus, leaving both Minni and another good friend named Adam Mattar behind in my Lagos apartment, arriving in Maiduguri the following day. This was the first time I saw my daughter

Nora - named after my late beloved sister, who was then about a year and a half.

It was wonderful and joyous family reunion. Eshaq was not able to bring the rest of my children with their mother because, according to him, they were schooling in Sudan, but also I felt because it would have taxed him more than he could afford.

I decided to settle in Maiduguri to be with my family and immediately started searching for a house to lease. A few days later I found a three room house at the center of the town and paid for a two year lease, then moved Hayat and the children to my new residence.

I rented an office at the main market and started a brokerage business, dealing mainly in currency exchange, but it was slow and frustrating and did not succeed. Yet more importantly, being in Maiduguri connected me to Darfur,we also had our seventh child Ibrahim in August 2000.

During this time, Minni remained in Lagos and engaged in business of his own, but by June 2000 he joined me in Maiduguri and declared his intent to return to Darfur to start the revolution we wanted. I was skeptical about his ability to execute such a project, but it turned out I was wrong. He started with others a work which has since changed Darfur and Sudan, perhaps forever.

In Abuja, June 2001 And Dr Khalil Ibrahim's Visit

After a couple of years in Maiduguri, it had become too difficult to support a family of nine people. Almost every Zaghawa trader failed me in my expectation of them. They were either afraid of being labeled as associate of opposition member when they return to Darfur, or sckeptical and felt a lack of guarantee as to the security of their money in my custody, or both.

In early February 2001, I consulted with Hayat, my nephew Abdulmagid and a few friends. We concluded it was best for me and my family that I find a regular job until things sorted out on the political front. The only thing I knew how to do was translation and interpretation. Though uncertain that I could get employment in Lagos or Abuja, I gave assurances to both of them and left for Lagos, where luckily I still maintained my apartment.

In Lagos, things were not easy, as I came back without money and Lagos was an expensive city, plus I needed to move a lot between different institutions until I got a job. At one point I resorted to selling some of my furniture and books to finance my movements. I applied to several institutions, mainly Arab embassies, excluding the Saudi Arabian, my former employers. I excluded them because I felt it would not augur well for me to return to them after honorably resigning.

It was several weeks before I got a single response. The replies were not encouraging. I had to get creative to secure a job, so I drew up an analysis on the political and economic situation of the country and presented them to the Moroccan Embassy. Luckily for me, the Ambassador was newly posted to the country and his political officer was unwilling to cooperate with him on writing things, such as analysis, so when I appeared in the scene with a detailed, competent analysis of the country, he welcomed my services. I realized later that I became a tool of intimidation in the hands of the ambassador against the insubordination of his counselor.

The ambassador invited me to his residence in Lagos, and after a brief meeting asked me to join the service at their new office in Abuja.

As the chances of getting employment increased, my domestic financial needs became more precarious. I sold more of my furniture and books, sometimes at give away prices, just to make enough to travel and relocate in Abuja and sustain myself for at least a month.

I arrived in Abuja on the morning of May 15th, 2001. This was my second visit to the new Federal Capital. The first was in early 1991 in company of a Saudi delegation at the height of first Gulf war between Saddam Hussein's forces and the coalition forces lead by the U.S. There was a huge difference between Abuja and Lagos. Abuja was new, clean and beautiful, with no crowds or traffic jams. The streets were well-planned and paved.

From the bus station I took a taxi cab to the Embassy. The ambassador received me and took me immediately to a room within the same building of the Chancery. He called an aide and asked him to get a bed and a mattress as quickly as possible and I moved into a room. It became a temporary accomodation for me for several months until I got my own apartment.

In early July, after two months on the job, I had two visitors. On a

Sunday morning, I had word from the security guard at the gate that two gentlemen were looking for me and that they said they were my brothers. I knew they must be Zaghawas, but wondered who or what they could be doing in Abuja, where no business of Zaghawa type thrived.

I went to the gate and greeted the tall, well-built man, bespectacled and light bearded, about my age or a bit younger. He was wearing a Chadian or Nigerian type of garment with an ivory colored turban which completely covered his head down to his chin. The other man was shorter and younger and wore a simple shirt and trousers. The older greeted me with a Sudanese embrace and in Zaghawa language, introducing himself as Khalil Ibrahim Mohammad, a medical doctor by training. He was a former minister of education in the greater Darfur state, but now in opposition to the government of Omar al-Bashir. He introduced his companion as Suliman, his aide.

It was exciting to meet such a personality and I immediately took them to the reception parlor in front of my room, where I prepared them sugary tea. Khalil was a marvelous conversationalist. He explained that he had been following our political activities in the SFDA, that he admired our efforts, and wanted to be part of the efforts to bring change in Sudan.

He went into detail of how he had become part of al-Bashir's government and how he fell out with him and his party when he discovered the true nature of the ruling Northern elite. He elaborated on the policies pursued by the Jallaba elite to perpetrate themselves in power and in control of national politics, wealth, public representation, and Sudanese identity. For them, Sudan means them and their community of Jallaba, while all other people within the geographical precincts of the country were considered either slaves or servants. Their plan was to pursue ethnic and cultural cleansing against all other groups in Sudan who opposed their stay in power, unless those groups accepted their policies and became part of their culture.

These were the same ideas we spent years speaking about and formed the SFDA and, before it, the DSJE and SSF, to achieve the changes necessary. What was new was that a person of his caliber and education, who was part of the Muslim Brotherhood and a member of National Islamic Front (NIF) could identify the facts and come out on the side of the opposition, like Daud Bolad before him. I felt he was sincere; he looked like a leader imbued with a purpose and a clear objective, and I admired that.

Khalil and his aid spent about two hours with me and then departed for their hotel. In the evening I visited them there and continued our conversation on Sudan. He explained he was in the process of forming an opposition political organization named Justice and Equity Movement. I suggested to him that instead of Justice and Equity, it could be Justice and Equality Movement. He liked the idea. I also gave him details of our earlier organization named the Democratic Solidarity for Justice and Equality (DSJE).

Khalil spent about a week in Abuja and then left for Chad. During his stay in Abuja, I also helped organize a meeting with the Nigerian authorities, where we explained the situation in Sudan, especially in Darfur. We were surprised that the senior Nigerian Foreign Affairs officials we met were nearly ignorant about the political situation in Northern Sudan. What they knew more about was the war in South Sudan.

A few months later, I returned to Maiduguri on a short vacation and made arrangements with Hayat to go back to Darfur and fetch the rest of our children. We also decided to keep and maintain the rented house in Maiduguri, until she returned with the children, especially since my nephew Abdulmagid was also there. It took another several months before Hayat and children returned.

It was like a rebirth when Abdulmagid phoned to tell me that Hayat was back from Darfur with the children. I was so eager to see my loved ones, especially Amal and Ahmed, whom I had not seen in six years, and Bishara and Aisha, whom I had not seen in four years. I waited for the weekend with eagerness and made my usual eight hour road journey to Maiduguri. The journey was smooth; I arrived in town ahead of schedule and headed straight to my house for our reunion.

CHAPTER FIFTEEN

The Garsalba Conference and Second Abeche Peace Talks

Around June 2002, Minni, whom I then called Suliman, called the Moroccan Embassy in Abuja from a location in Darfur to get in touch with me about his activity, but I missed his call as it came on a day I was not at the Embassy. He left me a satellite phone number.

I returned to Maiduguri the following weekend as usual to see my family and there met with Ahmed Yaaqob, Adam Bakhit, and Khatir Arko - all three former soldiers with both the Sudan army and Idris Déby's forces and members of the SFDA. We discussed Minni's call and speculated about the situation on the ground in Darfur, as well as about Minni's activity.

Weeks later, the three left Maiduguri separately for Darfur to meet Minni and the commanders, including Abdalla Abakar, Khatir Tourkhala, and others. They had transformed the opposition militia into organized opposition which was able to defend the villagers from attacks by both Arab militias and the regime's security forces.

Around the same time, Abdalla Domi also returned from the DR Congo and joined the revolutionaries. In March 2003, their new force launched attacks on their own upon government army units which were giving support to the militias which battled Fur villagers. In Golo and Toor, they distributed handwritten statements on their objectives. They also declared that they were part of the Sudan Federal Democratic Alliance (SFDA). It was a declaration which surprised many observers

The government went wild about the surfacing of this group in the area of Jebel Mara and started sending emissaries and mediators of Darfuri notables to the rebels to persuade them to lay down their arms. The rebels rejected the efforts.

The international media contacted Ahmed Ibrahim Diraige on the new development, but Diraige surprised the new rebels as well, along with me, Dr. Harir and others of the SFDA, by declaring in strong terms that he had nothing to do with the new rebel group, and that his forces were in Eastern Sudan and Eritrea. He added that the group has a leader, that leader is Abdulwahid Mohammad Nor, a young lawyer from Zalingi. This was the first time I heard the name Abdulwahid Nor.

Diraige made his statement in spite of my repeated previous phone calls to him and Dr. Harir informing them of the activity of this group in Jebel Marra as part of our SFDA, and that they needed guidance to the right political tactics rather than resorting to violence.

After the rebels heard Diraige's statement on the BBC, they changed the name of their group to the Darfur Liberation Front (DLF). I tried to call them on the new satellite phone number I was provided with and spoke with Arko Suliman Dahia, one of the prominent members of the group, and requested them moderation and to change the name to reflect a national objective for the struggle.

In the following weeks, that name changed to Sudan Liberation Army and later in the year, during the Garsalba Conference, the political cadre which associated themselves with the struggle formed the Sudan Liberation Movement. My friend Khalil Ibrahim's Justice and Equality Movement also appeared in full force, albeit just in the media.

The SLA went in to full operation in the Jebel Marra area, but mistrust developed between the Zaghawa commanders and the self-declared chairman of the SLA and later the SLM, Abdulwahid, which led to the withdrawal of the Zaghawa fighters from Fur areas of Jebel Marra to Dar Zaghawa of North Darfur. The fighters who moved to Dar Zaghawa were commanded by Abdalla Abakar and Minni Minnawi, who was now the self-proclaimed Secretary General of the SLA/SLM.

They were able to launch attacks on government military installations in North Darfur and liberate the whole of Dar Zaghawa in a matter of weeks. They set up their headquarters in the town of Kornoye, the birthplace of Abdalla Abakar and many other commanders.

In April 2003, a SLA force of about three hundred fighters launched a spectacular dawn raid on the military air base in Alfashir and destroyed seven warplanes before they were able to take off on attack missions against civilian and rebel targets. In the process, the commander of the air force, Air Vice Marshal Ibrahim Al-Bushra was captured by the rebels and taken prisoner. Al-Bushra was released after both his family and tribe appealed for mercy.

Meeting Domi in N'Djamena, September 2003

In October 2003, I made a major decision which would change the course of my life forever: I decided to leave for Darfur with Hayat and children-by now we had our eighth child Rashid, to be part of the struggle. I consulted with Hayat my decision and she expressed fear and worry, but I convinced her that in any case, we would be safe. We left Maiduguri in the early morning and arrived in N'Djamena late in the evening.

Arriving in Chad at the Cameroon border on the bridge side, we approached the check point that was apparently manned by Zaghawa speaking security personnel. I greeted them in Zaghawa and presented the Lassie Passé issued to us by a Zaghawa friend working with the Chadian consulate in Maiduguri. It was the use of the Zaghawa language, rather than the official document, that facilitated entry to the other side of the border

The only means of transportation from the border point into the city was either old, overcrowded buses or renting a motorbike at a higher cost. As it would be difficult for the children to ride the bikes, we opted for the crowded buses and headed straight to my in-laws' residence at Carte Andjarase.

At the house we were well received by the in laws. I met Hashim Derea Hayat's ancle who had recently returned from the USA, and other family members. I learned from Hashim that a delegation from the revolutionaries was in N'Djamena on the invitation by the government,and that Domi was with them.

They were accommodated in Mohammad Shawish's house not far

from where we were. The news made me feel as if there was a hand of Providence which directed me toward the common goal. That evening I had a good discussion with Hashim about the situation in Darfur and Sudan. I disclosed to him my plans behind coming to N'Djamena and my intention and resolve to proceed to Darfur to be part of the armed struggle.

Hashim was a man of revolting spirit against any form of injustice. He was happy I made such a decision, after being involved in the opposition so many years, and encouraged me to do my best to lead, because, as he put it, there was leadership vacuum in the field and almost all those in control lack any political experience. We agreed on almost every issue we tackled that evening and spent the better part of the following day in discussion on the advantages and disadvantages of my joining of the revolution.

Although I was eager to meet the delegation of the revolutionaries, I did not to go out from the house. Many visitors came day and night, and most of the talk was on the events in Darfur: the sporadic battles, the raid on Alfashir Airport in March 2003, and the courage of the young fighters commanded by Abdalla Abakar (Jorey Kitty).

On the evening of my third day in N'Djamena, Abdalla Domi and Omar Suliman, head of the delegation, came to see me. I had met Omar briefly years before. He was a former fighter who came to Chad with Déby's forces when they drove Hissein Habré out of power in November 1990. Like most of the Zaghawa youth of the border area who joined Déby's campaign those days, he remained and worked in N'Djamena for some time before going back to Sudan to be part of the revolution.

Beside their delegation, there were also a large number of wounded SLA fighters brought to N'Djamena for treatment. Both the military and the general hospitals were filled with the wounded warriors. Their visits were largely for courtesy for me and my family and the other members of the house, with whom Omar was also a relative.

I discussed my plans with Domi and was assured that things were in place for my entry into the field, and that a transport plane would be made ready for Tine. The following morning I bought the necessary blankets and mats that my family would need in Tine and which I needed in the desert in Darfur.

At Tine, October 2003

A colonel in the Chadian army was put in charge of the transport military plane. He was a rugged and stern looking officer who spoke Zaghawa in high-pitched tone. We boarded the plane with the delegation and other would-be SLM guests. These included people coming from other countries to attend the conference, among them Yusif Mahmoud Altyb, a resident of Kornoye and a cousin to Shartaye, the chief of Kornoye, Mohammad Imam, an ethnic Fur, and others.

Yusif Altyb and Mohammad Imam were members of the SFDA in Jeddah, Saudi Arabia. There were also some of those tired with the stagnation of the SFDA and were attempting to identify themselves with objectives of the SLM/SLA and associate with the young movement. There were other passengers, too: Chadian officials and their family members. Like all transport planes, there were few seats. Most of us squat on the plane floor with our luggage.

The trip to Tine took about three and a half hours. It was a smooth flight, and we arrived at the Chad Tine air strip a little before sunset. As we disembarked, a number of vehicles met us from the town. They were mostly Chadian local officials.

The air strip itself was a plain with hard level ground, between a large sand dune and rocky high ground. There were no houses or structures nearby and the two towns Tine Chad and Tine Sudan, separated only by a wadi, appeared in the distance with high minarets of mosques left and right.

We were transported to the town by some of the officials across the Valley of Tine, which forms the border between the two countries, to the other side of Tine. I had a nostalgic feeling of home coming after several decades away from Dar Zaghawa. This was the land I was born and raised in; now I returned after more than thirty years.

In Sudan Tine we lodged in a large building, said to be the former branch office of Sudatel, a Sudanese telecommunications company which provided telephone services to the local community before the conflict began.

My brother Eshaq also lived in town. His business had been based on the Sudan side of the town, but when the hostilities broke out, he was displaced and moved his family, like the rest of the business community, to the Chad part of the town. With the help of Domi and others, I was able to get a vehicle and take the family to Eshaq's house, and then returned to the SLA base that same night,and joined those newly coming to attend the conference.

We were well received by SLA personnel at the post, dislodged from the Sudanese army several months earlier after bloody clashes which left several dozen dead, mainly on the Sudanese army side. A meal of lamb and millet porridge was provided by the young fighters, followed by sugary tea. The night was cold and the winter of Zaghawa land had begun in earnest.

In the morning we had several visitors from the locals from across the valley and from the few people who still lived in the largely deserted town. Later in the day I strolled with Domi around the town, looking at the scars left by the fighting. By the time we returned, a decision was made for our departure that evening to Kornoye, the main town controlled by the SLA.

Among the local visitors was Baraka Hamid, an easy- going, simple man with baritone voice, whom I had little knowledge about, but it seemed that he had a great deal of knowledge about me and our previous political work. Baraka offered to be my escort and companion in my journey to Kornoye, the *de facto* headquarters of the SLA/SLM. Despite my reservation and disapproval and insistence that I held neither the means nor the authority to have any body as my companion, he joined us on the trip to Kornoye and lodged with us.

This occurred during a ceasefire period when the movement of both people and vehicles between Dar Zaghawa and the major cities of Darfur, especially Alfashir, were eased. I wished my mother and sisters, Aisha and Zarga, would come out of Alfashir to Tine, a prayer which was soon answered.

The Garsalba Conference, October 2003

Kornoye town now SLA/SLM heaquarters, was still bustling with life, although a larger number of its population has left to hide in the surrounding ravines and bushes for fear of attacks and air raids by the government forces. The market was still open, although fewer commodities were available. We lodged separately, while Yusif and Mohammad Imam went to Yusif's family home, which was also the Shartaye's house, who himself had fled to Alfashir like the rest of the Zaghawa traditional administrators. I went with Domi to a house of an SLA commander, where several other political leaders were also accomodated, but soon left for the Garsalba Valley for the conference. I notice big holes dug in the center of the house. Later I learned they were protection cover from Antenov bombs.

The Valley of Garsalba had very large, thick trees. It was thought that the recognizance flights and Antonov bombers of the Sudanese army would not be able to see from the air what was going on under the trees, hence the choice of the place for the conference.

Early in the moring a delegation from the organizing coming came in two vehicles to take us to the venue. They were chanting revolutionary slogans, and flying old Sudan flag of green blue and yellow, which also became the SLM/SLA flag afterwards. We met them out side of the house and was given the impression that I was their guest of honor. We travelled for quite some time on a rugged terrain. Upon arrival, we were met a little distance from where the rest of the gathering was by none other than my old friend Adam Shugar, who had returned to Sudan in the mid-nineties and became part of the local Sudanese politics before deciding to join the revolution in Darfur. We were both delighted to reunite again. With him was Mohammad Adam, a lawyer and legal adviser to the new SLA and the conference.

After the usual warm greetings, we were asked to undergo an oath taking procedure to be administered by the two. We obliged. We repeated after Mohammad Adam under the watch of Shugar very solemn and sacred words, that in essence committed us in no uncertain terms to the objectives of the resistance, which were the struggle to achieve justice, democracy, equality, rule of law, respect for human dignity, and respect for Sudanese cultures, languages, and ways of life.

Afterwards we moved to a gathering of SLA women delegates, who were singing praises of the revolution. We were asked by Shugar to address them and I delivered a speech. There were lots of cries of exultation from the women and firing of shots from SLA personnel using AK-47s.

From there we moved to the valley bed of Wadi Garsalba, where we met a large number of people in a meeting. Among the people very few did I recognize. It was a diverse gathering, Noteable among the gathered were Authman Bushra, Suliman Jamous, Hassan Mandella, Ahmed Kobor and others. They took turns making speeches, which were political in nature and highly articulate. They centered on how the revolution must be supported and advanced,but no one even by way of reference mentioned or made any reference to Sudan Federal Democratic Alliance SFDA.

After we made our speeches, some one suggested that we the new arrivals should also be taken to meet Minni Minnawi the secretary general, who was at another nearby location. We walked to the location and met Minni in full military fatigue and side pistol, with young looking body gaurds. His four wheel drive Toyota pickup vehicle, seized in a battle from Sudan military weeks earlier was covered with mud to camouflage it,was also in a shad beside them. He made a short speech in front of us and posed,then Authman Bushra cried out on top of his voice with a fist in the air *Thora! Thora!Thora Hata Nasrr(Revolution! Revolution! Revolution! Till victory!)* and all repeated after him. After that we left Minni to our shade where more speeches were made. We also learned that Abdalla Abakar, the commander general of the SLA forces, had been there the previous day and delivered a very powerful speech.

Abdalla Abakar was an indigene of Dar Galla of Dar Zaghawa. He was born and brought up in Kornoye in the early seventies. In the late eighties he dropped out of school, went to Libya, became part of Gaddafi's revolutionary forces and trained in various heavy weaponry, then later joined Idriss Déby's force when the latter rebelled. He served and excelled in Déby's army afterward. Until Diraige's declaration on the BBC in March 2003, he was at the core of the SFDA and a very humble man. Only sheer necessity forced him to assume the mantle of leadership.

Abdalla Abakar's speech at the conference, which was recorded, was a rare piece of Zaghawa eloquence. It was a speech which revealed for the first time the structural relationship between Minni as Secretary General (therefore higher in the hierarcy) and Abdalla Abakar as SLA Commander, and the hitherto undeclared ambition of Minni to play a major role at the national level.

It was due to the outcome of this conference that the Sudan Liberation Movement (SLM) was formally formed as the political wing of the resistance in Darfur. Minni Minnawe's designate became the secretary general. The group of the founding members was referred to in Kornoye as the political committee, and thereafter the two became two wings of an organization, referred to as SLA/SLM

The SLA/SLM sector in Northern Darfur was referred to by the Khartoum regime as the Kornoye group, while the southern sector was referred to as the Jebel Marra group. The northern sector operated under the joint command of Abdalla Abakar and Suliman Arko Minnawi, who later adopted, as mentioned earlier, his nick name Minni as his official name.

Each sector operated independently of the other, especially after the Zaghawa group moved out of Jebel Marra due to mistrust. There was no or little coordination between them, militarily or politically. While Abdulwahid held fort in the hills of Jebel Marra and waged a media campaign against the regime, the SLA northern sector waged a different campaign. It engaged government armies in sporadic battles in Tine, Abgamra, Gorbo Jong, Maleet,Kutum, Disa, Kulbus, and Jerjira.

The belief of each and every SLA fighter was that the revolution was unstoppable. It would sweep everyone into oblivion and establish a new era in Khartoum and Sudan. There was no mention of Darfur, rather a change in Khartoum.

Because the fighters under Abdalla Abakar and Minni had tested the Sudanese army in many pitched battles and close fights, they realized they had the higher fighting spirit and raw courage; but little did they realize that wars are fought not only with big guns but also - and most importantly - with resources and economic might and the support of the people.

Abdalla Abakar and his chief commanding officers such as Joma Hagar, Ahmed Torkhala, Bakhit Karima, Adam Bakhit, Ahmed Yaaqob, Jodo Isa (Saqur) and others were men of rare courage. While Abdalla Abakar set the example of heroic resolve for the sake of the motherland, the others were not found lacking in most of his qualities.

It was Adam Bakhit who conceptualized the idea of the raid on Alfashir Airport to destroy the planes even when we were in Maiduguri, which was later executed by the group led by Abdalla Abakar.

Jodo Isa (Saqur) led the campaign in East and South Darfur. Jodo's military exploits saved the SLA from total collapse and disintegration and also ridiculed Omar Albashir, who declared in January 2004 that the rebellion was crushed and the military operations in Darfur had ended.

Shortly after Albashir's declaration, SLA forces struck Towisha, Motawarid, Tawila, Tarne and Shearia, with heavy losses on the government forces. Immediately after this SLA made a counter statement on BBC declaring that the SLA/SLM now controlled even larger and more economically important areas than before.

Reflecting on the Ruins in Geli Njogot

Several days after the conference, Minni offered me the opportunity of accompanying him with his father to visit his home village Geli Njogot, which was also used to be my own village in early sixties. Baraka came with us despite my disapproval and explanation that I was in charge of nothing on that trip. We rode in two vehicles, one an SUV type seized from the government was carrying Minni and me and three or four of his body gaurds, and another a 4x4 toyta pickup truck carrying Minni's father and Baraka with other SLA personnel.

We made first to Foraweya, a small town where I had first gone to school in the early sixties. Despite the lapse of almost four decades, Foraweya did not change much, except the village grew in size, but the school remained the same. Classrooms were still built of straw and wood as in the sixties. Yet now the scars of war were everywhere. The school was totally destroyed.

It was there we met the SLM women's chapter leader, Aisha Nor Ali Hassan,the daughter of Nor Ali Hassan who petitioned the government on the murder of his half brothers Mahmud and Bakhit in 1991. Aisha is a woman of great courage and generosity.

From Foraweya we proceeded to Geli Njogot and arrived late in the evening. A lamb was slaughtered for us by the few residents we met and we enjoyed our night eating roasted meat and drinking sugary tea. Minni's father was nostalgic of our days together in the village, and spoke about some of the good qualities of my father,whom he knew since their childhood.

The next morning I woke up very early. I seized the opportunity to visit the spot where my family home used to be some thirty-five years ago, just to be by myself and do some meditation and reflect on childhood memories. It was only some few hundred yards from Uncle Arko's house.

I was able to locate the area, even the very spots where the huts of my parents used to be, even though there was not a single trace of the large stones which were used to construct the walls. I was astonished at the disappearance of every single stone. The only remaining trace was the grinding stone which my mother used to grind millet and other cereals to make flour for food.

This was the place where I was first sent to school in 1962 and also a place my family had some of its most difficult and turbulent years. It saw a turning point in the life of my family in 1965, beginning with the rift between mother and father and differences between him and Abdelkarim – also known as Edeh, my father's first son and *de facto* second in charge of the family herds.

Edeh was a youth of seventeen or eighteen at the time, a period when a Zaghawa person transitions from childhood to manhood. He had his own ambitions at becoming an independent man, but those ambitions conflicted with Father's plans, resulting in serious and often violent disputes between them. Edeh ran away from the family, abandoning many responsibilities and, as it was often the case with youths in his situation, had gone to the Nile region of Central Sudan and never returned. It was in our last days in this village that we lost every semblance of unity and cohesion.

As these and other thoughts crossed my mind, I heard a noise behind me. It was Minni. We moved around the village, which was beginning to wake up. At the spot where it used to be a dancing arena in the olden days, I began a discussion about the great revolutionary men in history, from Mao Tse-tung of China, to Fidel Castro of Cuba; from George Washington of America to the African freedom fighters, such as Nelson Mandela, Jomo Kinyata Samora Michelle and others. I talked about the great warriors in history, from the knights of Europe in the Middle Ages to the Japanese Samurai; from Alexander the Great and Bonaparte to the great commanders which fought in World War I and II.

The message in all this discourse, which was a reiteration of earlier discourses I made in Lagos with Minni and others throughout the years of the struggle, was the necessity of perseverance in the struggle.

Toward the afternoon we proceeded to other villages and areas where SLA personnel were and where some of the local population took refuge from government aerial bombardment. We concluded our tour by the evening and returned to Kornoye, leaving Uncle Arko in his village. Baraka Hamid was also peremptorily ordered by one of Minni's top body guards to leave our company.

The Abeche Ceasefire Renewal Talks, November 2003

Not quite a week from the conclusion of the Garsalba conference and drafting the final resolutions by a special committee in a retreat in a secluded village, we held a meeting of what was then referred to as political committee in Kornoye, which was in essence the political wing of the resistance.

We were later joined by Minni in the night with a retinue of body guards who seemed to be around him to give him protection as a leader and also to give him confidence and an air of authority and may be also intimidation. We had a heated discussion and a decision was reached that the political committee of the SLM would head to Tine the following day, where a delegation would be selected from the SLM and SLA to travel to Abeche in Chad to meet the government delegation and present and negotiate what was by then termed and refered to by Chadian authorities as supplements/annexes to the first Abeche ceasefire agreement of September 2003. Those were, in effect, the SLA/SLM political demands for the Khartoum government to stop the fighting or lay down arms.

The next morning as we prepared to leave for Tine, the commander general of SLA forces, Abdalla Abakar, also came with several vehicles with light artilary and automatic weapons mounted on them. It was the first time I met Abdallah and my first impression of him was that he was a likeable figure. A young man in his early thirties, of average height and build, his facial features were less severe than I imagined. He greeted me and the others with a firm handshake and a deep voice.

As I tried to introduce myself, he said he was aware of who I was and that Minni talked a lot about me. Shortly after Abdallah's arrival, Minni also arrived with his body gaurds and he taunted Abdalla as to the size of the body guard force he had with him at the time. We had a full convention of the leadership. Now I fully realized, that this is a new order of things,a new administration for the liberated areas with governors and police,and courts system,a new command and control structure very different from what we worked for or anticipated. There was no mistake the two were in charge and working in great harmony. Where would I fit in such a structure was not clear to me. Our meeting did not last long as the two of them left separately; Minni confirmed that he would meet us again in Tine the next day.

The following day the political committee left Kornoye for Tine and we arrived late afternoon, encamping in Khatir Hamid Dhay's house in the heart of the town. We spent the rest of the day and evening discussing our demands and the strategy of the negotiations with the government. We divided the demands between political and economic issues, but before that we insisted that a conducive environment must be created by the government prior to beginning of any serious negotiations. That included, among other things, the disarmament of the Janjaweed militia, allowing unfetered access to humanitarian aid, and international observation of the talks.

Top on political demands was self-rule for the Darfur region within the larger Sudanese state and rotation of the Sudan presidency among the regions. Economically, our demands (later termed "wealth sharing" after the terminology of the Naivasha comprehensive peace agreement between the Sudan government and Sudan Liberation Movement) included equitable sharing of developmental projects in Sudan and that Darfur must be accorded affirmative action.

Mini Joined us in Tine, and presented a list of the delegation to the talks,comprising the two wings, the SLM and the SLA. One of the very vocal members of the political committee Suliman Jamos was also excluded from the list. Mini's explanation was that Jamos was a well known member of Popular Conference party of Hassan Alturabi,therefore his appearance with the delegation In Abeche will put a lot of question marks,as to the movement's relationship with Alturabi. As for the head of the delegation he left it for us to work it out. Someone from the military wing suggested that Abdalla Domi should head us and was seconded.

Towards mid day of October 26 2003 the Chadian government plane arrived to pick us From Tine and we arrived in Abeche on the evening, two days before the expiry date of the September ceasefire. The official delegation of the negotiators was comprised of seventeen people, ten in their political capacity representing the SLM and three representing the SLA military command,and four security personel. The ten were Abdalla Domi, Hassan Mandela, Ahmed Kobor, Mohammad Imam, Adam Shugar, Authman Bushra. Others were Bahar Arabie, Jarelnabi Abdelkarim, Mohammad Adam, and Suliman Marajan. The three representing the SLA military command were Isa Musa Jery, Mohammad Abdalla Khamis (Kobeh), and Adam Suliman (Toba). The later was a close relative of president Deby,but also was born and raised in central eastern Sudan. His presence in the delegation or even in the SLA military was a puzzle to me,as his younger brothers were also working with the president's security and body guards.

We arrived Abeche in the early hours of the evening and were well received by the Chadian authorities. We also learned that Chadian president himself was in town to facilitate the talks. We were taken to a villa with a large compound and lodged there. Later in the evening a delegation of three Chadian officials visited us. It included Mohamat Salih Adam Jaro,my guest in Lagos in 1989. They asked if we brought the suppliments/annexes to Abeche agreement of September 2003. We did not give a definite answer and they left rather unhappy about our answers. We held a meeting afterwards and made a plan for the following mornings talks. We decide that only four people should talk to the government side after the opening remarks. The four were Ahmed Kobor(a Rezegat) Hassan Ibrahim Mandela(a Falata)Authman Bushra (a Zaghawa)and Adam Shugar (Zaghawa). The following morning the talks were officially opened. The Sudan government delegation was headed by the Chief of State Security Service and also included the governor of North Darfur and the commander of western military command.

Domi read our opening remarks. They were very militant and strong. Both the Sudan government delegation and our host government were eager to rush us to sign an immediate peace agreement, where the SLA/SLM would commit itself to laying down its arms and accept cantonment of its forces in designated areas under the supervision of a joint ceasefire commission which comprised the three parties.

The SLM/SLA delegation immediately saw the danger of committing itself to such an agreement, which in any case it was not mandated to conclude, and started playing tactics until it got another extension of the ceasefire and could return to the field to consult with the commanders.

To achieve this, the delegation refused to present its demands and insisted on more time to prepare.

The talks dragged on for about a week, during which time President Idriss Déby closely followed their progress, or lack of it. He held several consultation meetings with select members from the two delegations. I noticed that I was clearly sidelined from the meetings with president,or even perhaps unwelcome to the talks.

The Chadian general who was assigned as a facilitator expressed on several occasions his hatred of Minni Minnawi, and accused Minni of seeking help from John Garang, the SPLA/SPLM leader, to carry out the war in Darfur. At a point I countered the general and reminded him that if he or his government hated Minni, then there was no point or reason why an SLM/SLA delegation should be in Abeche or Chad for that matter, because in such event his government looked biased. The general suddenly became nervous and very quiet and left us.

The following days we saw no more of him. Eventually SLA/SLM got what it wanted and the ceasefire was extended for another month. After the talks we were transported to Tine by road with a large Chadian military convoy scorting us. On arrival to our base in Tine, we went into all night long meeting. We evaluated our talks with the government side and discussed the strategy a head. Mini joined us in the morning and discussions continued.

CHAPTER SIXTEEN

Casualties of War

As the end of the ceasefire period approached, the Chadian government again prepared for the meeting of the two sides of the Peace Talks. Early in the morning of November 26th, 2003, a plane arrived Tine from N'Djamena to pickup the SLA/SLM delegation, which the Chadian government insisted must involve Mini and Abdalla Abakar, but we decided that the two should not be with the delegation. The membership of the delegation we selected was largely made up of the same people who attended the second Abeche talks.

The Chadian official who came with the plane was the same army general with whom I had the argument during the second Abeche talks. He was clearly upset that there was no sign of Abdalla Abakar or Minni. He insisted that his instructions were primarily to pick up the two men, but we also insisted that we represented the movement and it would make no difference whether Minni and Abdalla were present or not, and in any case both of them were far away from Tine at that particular moment.

He was left with the choice: either pick us or depart without our delegation. He grew nervous and made some calls to N'Djamena. He was instructed to proceed to N'Djamena with the delegation, but it was not clear whether he was instructed to exclude me from the delegation or made the decision himself. The attempt was naïve, and in any case could not have served to influence the decision of the SLA/SLM to lay down the arms or not. He called Domi and Shugar aside and after some discussion, both Shugar and Domi acted in a way which I considered even more naïve. They said it would be better if I remained behind. I needed no explanation why, but my surprise stemmed from the two of them accepting the Chadian request. The plane departed without me.

On the evening of November 28th, 2003, two days before the end of the Abeche Ceasefire, there were calls from top officials to Minni and Abdallah to join the delegation and that the plane would be sent the following morning once again to Tine to pick them. Minni accepted but Abdalla remained behind. He came to Tine with his body guards late in the night and camped on the out skirts of the town.

The following morning we met him at the SLA police post. I explained how I was excluded from the rest of the delegation and that if my staying behind served the cause, I would remain behind, but he insisted that I must be at the talks.

We rode together to the airstrip and met the same general waiting. Again, he made an attempt to stop me, but this time I argued vehemently with him. I told him in no uncertain terms that these talks were between Sudanese parties and not between us and his government, and added that he could take to N'Djamena whomever he likes but without me, they would not find any solution to the problem.

This seemed to both infuriate and bewilder him more, at one point Minni intervened with one sentence: "He cannot be excluded." The general's demeanor changed and he kept aside while we boarded the aircraft.

Upon arrival at N'Djamena we were met by top security officials and their retinue. Three vehicles were brought to us. The general made an attempt to put me and Minni in separate vehicles, but we forced our way into the same vehicle.

First we were taken to the guest house where the rest of the delegation which came earlier the previous day was lodging. The general then had a change of mind and came rushing from where he had been talking on the phone to where Minni and I were sitting. He informed Minni that he was to stay somewhere else. To his chagrin, I came along.

The other accommodation was quite a distance from the villa where the main delegation stayed and was much smaller. There were three rooms and a large living room. Minni and his body guards occupied two rooms while I took the third one.

At around eleven o'clock when we were preparing to go to bed, three top Chadian army generals who were close to President Déby arrived. They included General Esakha Deyar - the same Deyar who spent some time with me in Lagos in my house in 1989 - Omar Bahar, and Hery Tayara. They asked Minni to go with them in closed-door meeting. Minni obliged but later asked me and Bakhit Hamid, another member of the SLA/SLM delegation who came with us, to be present in the meeting.

Hery Tayara said they were sent by the president to discuss our plans with the government delegation. Deyar continued the discussion. He was famous for being very eloquent in the Zaghawa language and I believe at no other time than that night he tried to prove his eloquence, as the issues he tried to tackle were enormous and complicated and needed great deal of vocabulary in Zaghawa to articulate them.

General Deyar, who did not highlight the recognition of my past relationship with him, went into detail of Chadian rebellions and rebel stories, drawing analogies between the Darfur resistance and Chadian rebel stories, which most ended either in peace making and power-sharing with the government or annihilation of the rebellion by the government. He ended on the note that Sudan was huge country with enormous resources; its government has a strong army which could not be crushed by a rebel force; and that it is best for the SLA/SLM to make peace immediately.

He spoke for about forty minutes or so, then General Bahar, too, spoke along the same lines. When the three stopped to hear our reaction, Minni did not speak much, but he said there were clear differences between the Chad rebellion and Darfur revolution, and in any case he was not the one to decide the fate of the revolution at that moment. The delegation would make the decision. I emphasized what he had said, adding what was going on in Darfur was more than a mere rebellion of the Chadian style. The closest comparison is with Chad's FROLINAT and the Sara dominated government of the sixtieswhich ended with the victory of the forces that comprised FROLINAT.

No clear understanding was reached with the generals and they returned to the president to relay the issue. As we prepared to go to bed again, the same generals returned to inform us that the president wanted to see us immediately. We hurriedly dressed in the best we had and drove with the generals to the presidential villa.

We entered a large, well-furnished living room and met more generals already seated. There was also a large sofa decorated with Chadian coat of arms on one end of the room, apparently a presidential seat. We took our seats and waited. Within a short time the rest of our delegation was also brought in from where they were lodged.

About half an hour later, the president walked in and everybody stood up. He was casually dressed in an Arab-type garment and was in a light mood. He shook hands with the members of our delegation before sitting on the large sofa with the coat of arms.

He spoke about the role he played in the revolts and rebellions which took place in Chad and reminded us that each rebellion ended in a peace agreement and share of political power. He also went in to details of the efforts exerted by his government to end the rebellion in Darfur, concluding that his efforts were not appreciated by either party. Therefore, he declared, he was withdrawing from mediation because neither party was serious about stopping the war and achieving the peace.

We tried to persuade him to change his mind, but he was adamant. He informed us that a plane will be made available the following morning to convey our delegation to Tine, and with that he ended the meeting.

The next day, we waited to be taken to the airport, but the plane was not ready. It was almost evening before vehicles were sent to take us to the airport. We boarded a military transport plane for Tine. What happened to the government delegation, or whether there was a government delegation in N'Djamena at all, we couldn't say, as we did not meet them.

South Wadi Sayera and Evolving a Spirit of Camaraderie

We arrived Tine at approximately eight o'clock in the evening. It was stark night and every one worried whether the plane could locate the air strip and land safely. As the plane circled the town several times, it became obvious that the pilot couldn't locate the ends of the runway.

SLA members on the ground also realized the dilemma of the pilot and quickly lined up their vehicles on both sides of the airstrip, turning on their head lights to indicate the ends of the airstrip. The pilot made a bold attempt to land, which was extremely risky to our lives and touched down with a lot of turbulence, causing minor injuries and bruises to many of us.

We thanked God and even congratulated each other for making it alive as we disembarked. We departed immediately to our side of Tine, where we lodged as usual in Khatir Hamid Dhay's derelict house. We were served with dinner of porridge and meat by the Tine SLA/SLM committee, with whom Eshaq was a member.

The following morning we held a political leadership meeting to discuss the strategy a head. Like most of our meetings, it was rowdy one, where divergent views were put across. Some advocated that the armed wing must subordinate itself to the political wing, while others advocated that all must forget their former political affiliations and commit themselves to SLM/SLA goals and objectives, which were the establishment of a just system in Sudan, a system which recognizes and accepts the cultural diversity of its peoples, advocates the equitable share of power and wealth, and trains all in military and self-defense strategies.

In the end it was agreed that all political committee members, which were in effect the SLM branch of the resistance, must move to South Wadi Sayra where commander Abakar was based and stay in a secluded retreat. An incident also happened, Authman Bushra objected to the idea that all political committee should head to South Wadi Sayra. He wanted to stay behind in Tine, or go to Kornoye but he was pressurized or perhaps threatened to come a long with the team. Vehicles were made ready and we all traveled to South Wadi Sayra. We arrived in early hours of the night.

The place itself seemed to be a thick, tropical forest with huge acacia trees which covered the sky, while beneath them grew long reeds and weeds. As we approached, Several camp fires flickered through the thick forest, but no one was certain which one was the commander's fire.

The next morning, Abdalla Abakar came to meet us, accompanied by Yahya Hassan Neil (who at the time acted like a second in command). He was in casual military uniform, and several guards following on both sides. He apologized for not visiting us earlier. He stayed close to an hour, joking and sipping tea with us.

Life was simple in our forest retreat and a spirit of camaraderie evolved among many of us, despite the differences in our former political affiliations and opinions. We met every other evening, if no air strikes were carried out on our location or nearby with thunderous sound, to propose and discuss ideas.

Although each and every one of us had taken oath to leave behind his former political loyalties and beliefs and be a loyal and dedicated member of the SLM, many of us behaved in a manner incompatible with the oath he had taken, which caused conflict with the movement's intelligence and security operatives.

We were such a lot of contradicting political backgrounds and beliefs that we spent much time strategizing, planning and debating our differences. Each tried to establish the merits of his views and ideas and demonstrate that he had better leadership attributes. Most of our meetings were in no way relevant to the urgency of the situation we were in; few had real appreciation of our perilous circumstances.

Some freely made phone calls to former colleagues in the government who were still in Khartoum or to people with contacts with both the government and Janjaweed leaders, thereby revealing some of our closely guarded secrets and risking the exposure of our location to government intelligence.

About two weeks in our camp we were joined by defectors from Khartoum, some of them like Adam Alnour seemed to me very genuine revolutionaries, others I suspected them and disliked them.

One such call was made to a certain Musa, a Janjaweed chief in Khartoum. This was immediately after an attack by government forces where the Janjaweed in the Kulbos area was repulsed by SLA forces. The caller's reasoning was that we must open communication with the Janjaweed to bring them over to our side, or at least neutralize them.

It was a stupid and extremely dangerous thing to do and I strongly objected, but the old fellow had already managed to convince the SLA commander Abdalla Abakar and some other commanders on the imperative of meeting with the representatives of the Janjaweed in a nearby location. Abdalla agreed to the plan, the details of which were kept under raps from most of us.

As later revealed, its purpose was that the Janjaweed would defect to the SLA in mass. In the initial stage they would send about five hundred of their fighters to join SLA ranks, with the rest following after a deal was struck between SLA leadership and their leadership. The Janjaweed leader insisted that any agreement must be reached with Abdalla Abakar himself personally and in his presence.

It was obvious to me and to others of our members that all was not well with such an arrangement.

On the appointed day, a delegation departed early in the morning to the locality of Maon, headed by Bushra. It had as its members two men of Shaigia orgin, Ali Abdelrahim, a former Libyan revolutionary committees veteran who came to SLA following Bushra; and Adil Mahjub, better known as Adil Tayara,a bespectacled man whom I always innerly suspected to be a secret agent. He claimed to have defected from NDA in Asmara and came to Khartoum and made peace with government, again defected from the government to joined the SLM; others were Mohammad Imam a Fur; Mohammad Abdalla Khamis (Kobi); and a guide who knew the agreed location of the meeting. Commander Abdalla Abakar himself,left in two vehicles of bodyguards following a separate route from the one followed by Bushra's group.

A few hours to their departure, two Antonov bombers appeared right above our camp and hovered along the route taken by Abdalla Abakar. They circled the area for several hours.

Bushra's group communicated with the Janjaweed group through satellite phones. According to their account, each time the Janjaweed called, they wanted to make sure Abdalla Abakar was with them. As the two SLA/SLM groups approached the location from different directions, the Janjaweed requested a delay when the bombers appeared over head. Another request was made for more delay until it was evening, then nightfall.

An attack then occurred in our vicinity in the same evening on Zaghawa herders by Janjaweed. More than seven herds of sheep and camel were taken with their herders. A call for SLA rescue came from the herd owners and locals, a situation which made Abdalla Abakar open hitherto temporarily suspended communications with other SLA commanders and gave instructions for the rescue of the herders and the herds.

Bushra and the group began to suspect that there was an element of Trojan horse in the scheme and began to move back to the base. Two SLA companies set out to retrieve the herds. By the time they closed in with the abductors the next morning, they came under heavy artillery bombardment from a government force which snuck into the area. The SLA force fought back but was able to recover only about half of the herds and none of the herding boys. As the SLA force headed towards our camp another government force appeared,just less than a kilometer from us,a battle took place. The government force withdrew to head towards Abgamra.

At the base we discussed the issue and found many faults to the plan of meeting the Janjaweed leaders and prayed for the safe return of the two groups.

Abdalla Abakar and Bushra returned to base toward the afternoon. Both were angry that the mission turned out to be futile and a farce, and a naïve effort by Bushra to win the Janjaweed to our side. It was a dangerous attempt which could have cost them their lives if not for the incident of abduction.

I visited Abdalla at his camp immediately after their return and found him in a bad mood, not ready to talk about the events of the previous day. Instead he cracked jokes with his subalterns and bodyguards and busied himself with calls to his commanders.

Abdalla Abakar the Martyr

The morning of December 22nd or 23rd, two days after the return of Authman Bushra and the group which accompanied him on the mysterious journey to meet the Janjaweed leaders,we were in our usual spot, Some were discussing the events of the previous three days and some were drafting political statements.

Bushra was talking on the phone reporting to Amnesty International about the Janjaweed attacks on herders and the kidnapping of herder boys in Maon area, when suddenly a snake appeared and entered between his legs, forcing him to leap frog clumsily to avoid what could have been a fatal bite. The snake slithered toward us, creating panic and unsettling many of us. We tried to hit the venomous creature with sticks and stones but it escaped in to the thick grass.

We continued our discussions when I spotted Abdalla walking towards us, dressed in a very unusual manner. For the first time I saw him, and I believe the others did, too, in civilian dress, with a small civilian white cap on his forehead. As he approached us, he changed direction and walked away in a circular manner.

He was followed by two bodyguards. One was holding his satellite phone and the other, Ishmael Andolok, carried his pistol and followed at some distance. He strolled among the trees for about half an hour, as if in self-meditation, and then came to us. He stood very close to me and asked, with softness in his voice, whether I had unspent dry battery cells for a small nine-band radio receiver. I told him I did and reached for my bag to hand him the battery, but he walked away, leaving Andolok to collect the battery.

It was apparent that he was a man in deep thought and some kind of ominous premonition troubled him. The others I believe were totally oblivious about his and my feelings. A short a while later, I made for Abdalla's camp and met him again, this time wearing his usual camouflage military fatigue. His boys prepared his usual roasted meat and millet porridge meal.

I approached him but he was on phone with Minni, bitterly complaining about leakage of secret SLA plans to government intelligence. Although his food was made ready, he did not sit down to eat. He just kept on smoking his cigarettes and drinking and made more calls to sector commanders.

Not quite an hour later, Abdalla left the camp with almost all his bodyguards in a great hurry. He left no clue as to where he was heading. We thought he might have gone to one of the other camps of his forces.

Toward the evening news began to filter in from the calls we made to other commanders. We were informed that the government offensive had begun and an attack was expected on Abgamra, and that Abdalla Abakar had gone there to see the preparations for the defense of the area. From our base to Abgamra was a distance of about seventy miles, and with the SLA fighters driving style, the distance could be covered in less than two hours. Abakar reached Abgamra and camped with the SLA force there. With the government forces already in sight, he prepared for a counter offensive the next morning.

From the account we heard later, Abakar delivered his attack as the government force was preparing to move against his position. It was a fierce, sporadic battle, where SLA fighters, in their close and fast strategy, fought with devilish fury and descended on the trenches of government forces to flush them out.

As the battle raged, government forces were reinforced by air cover.

Antonov bombers and helicopter gunships came to the rescue of their seriously beaten force. The gunships made for the location of Abakar and fired rockets and machine gun shots at his personal vehicle. The gunner on his vehicle's machine gun was killed. Abakar took over and returned fire at the gunships. Again the gunship fired at his vehicle, wounding him in the abdomen and the thigh, while the vehicle was partially destroyed.

It was obvious that the gunships identified his vehicle and targeted him. A number of SLA commanders and fighters in the battlefield, including Joma Haqar his deputy, came to his aid. He was carried off the battlefield and immediately transported to Kornoye. All the way to Kornoye, a distance of about eighty miles, he was conscious and his usual self, but on arrival his condition deteriorated.

We made several attempts to get in contact with him that day but to no avail. I tried Minni also but both their phones kept connecting our calls to their voice mail answering services.

No one among us had an inkling to what happened to the beloved young Commander General. People went on doing their normal activities, but toward the evening we were subjected to a massive bombardment by Antonovs and the bombs began to fall closer.

That same evening we were visited by an SLA logistics officer by the name commader Morsal. He confirmed that Commander Abdalla Abakar was wounded and carried to Kornoye, but he also assured us that the wound was not life threatening. The logistics officer himself headed for Kornoy,and adviced us to remain in constant contact with him through his satellite phone. He used to call us almost on hourly basis to brief us about the developments on the ground,the movements of Janjaweed and government troops. On the way,very close to Kornoy he made very last call informing us about his safty concerns. His voice was faint almost whispering, then no more. We tried frantically to reach him,but we could not. He was abushed by a government force with Janjaweed and killed.

The news about commander Abdalla was worrisome news to us all, but we kept assuring ourselves that all would be well. Early the next morning, calls started coming in from all directions, especially from the international media, all trying to verify the story of the wounded commander, which was immediately leaked by government intelligence. We confirmed that he was wounded in battle, but also I kept denying that his wound was life threatening and that he had been treated and returned to his normal duties.

At the same time, Abdulwahid got in touch with people in our sector and had assurances that Abakar's injury was not serious, so he also made statements to the media concurring with our statements. Yet a couple of days later, Abakar's condition grew serious due to lack of proper medical attention, as there were no hospitals or qualified doctors in areas controlled by the SLA. One opinion was to carry him to Tine in Chad where the international Doctors Without Borders-MSF had established a field hospital to treat the victims of war in Darfur, but before anything could be done, he passed away in the presence of most of the senior military commanders of the SLA.

When I received the news, I immediately called Minni to keep the news from the media at least for a while to maintain the morale of the fighters, but Minni said the story was already leaked to the media and there was no use denying it.

As the commanders prepared to bury the body of their leader, government warplanes stepped up their raids on Kornoye. Various bombers – Antonovs and MiG 27s - took part in the attacks, resulting in heavy casualties among civilians. In the confusion, someone sent a statement to the NDA opposition radio, known then as *Radio Voice of Sudan*, to the effect that SLA high command had appointed Adam Abu shanap as Commander General to succeed Abdalla Abakar.

Immediately after the story broadcast, We called Minni for the explanation of this rather strange story but Minni was unaware of it. Later it was agreed among the leadership of SLA that Haqar, Abakar's deputy, must take over as Commander General. A correction story was sent to the *Radio Voice of Sudan*.

Our camp became largely empty after the death of Abdalla Abakar, as teams of SLM from among our number were dispatch to the eastern parts of the SLA-controlled areas of Jebel Midop and Bir Maza. There remained only five senior members of the SLM/SLA out of about fifteen, as well as some fighters and the radio communication equipment with its two operators. We were highly vulnerable to attacks from the air and possibly by the ground, especially after it became apparent that our camp had become a known target to the government air force.

The Antonov bombers daily hovered overhead and dropped bombs some times just a few yards from the spot where we slept at night and had our camp fire. I was the first to notice this danger and communicated my concern to my colleagues. Some took it seriously while others tried to play it down.

As decisions in our group were always made in a democratic manner, I requested the camp should be moved to a more tactically secure place. Shugar and Adam Alnur agreed with me, but Bushra and Mandela wanted to defer the move for a day or two. The moment we were supposed to move out, they left for a near by village on an entirely different matter. We seized the opportunity afforded by their absence and moved camp to a location about ten miles away, taking with us their belongings. At the expected time of their return, we sent a vehicle to pick them from the old camp site. When they arrived, they expressed their delight on our choice of the new location.

A few days after our relocation, I received a call from Minni saying he had received a call that a USA government envoy would be on the Sudan Chad border shortly to assess the humanitarian situation, and that the envoy would like to meet a representative from the SLM/SLA. He suggested that I meet the envoy along with Yahya Hassan Neil. I agreed to the plan and set out one early morning with Abdelmajid Wadi for Tine in an SLM vehicle, leaving the rest of the group behind. We arrived Tine in record time and lodged at the SLM/SLA base in town.

A few hours from my departure, our new location came under attack by a large government force with Janjaweed militia. It was only under a great deal of defensive firing from the few body guards in the group that they were able to ward off the attack and withdraw to another safe location.

At Tine we could not meet the American envoy as I arrived late. It seemed he was in a great hurry and could wait no longer for our arrival. We learned that he toured the makeshift camps of the refugees who crossed to the Chad side of the border, and then he left. That same day the town was also subjected to massive bombardment by the Sudan air force, resulting in the death and injury of many people and destruction of many houses. The following morning, not quite five minutes after I left the hut I slept in the previous night to an SLM location, was struck buy a bomb, totally destroying it. I thanked my stars for that hair breadth scape. Raids continued for the rest of the day. The situation in other twons of Dar Zaghawa,Dor,Omborow,Mozbed,and Kornoy was even worse.

Hell Let Loose Upon Civilians, December-January 2003

It was a Friday morning when I crossed the border to Tine in Chad with other SLM personnel to get the Chadian local population's reaction to the mayhem which was going on right at their doorstep. We went to several locations and ended at the market, which by now had a majority of Darfuri traders, relocated from the other side of the border. The market was also adjacent to a large mosque said to be built with the assistance of the Chadian president.

The situation on our side of the border was the talk of the town and the market. The battles between advancing government forces supported by Janjaweed and SLA continued in Jirjira town. The sound of heavy guns fire and aerial bombardment from the battle ground at Jirjira twon continued. People were horrified and angry, but there was little they could do to stop the killings. Their sympathy with the people of Darfur was obvious.

In the afternoon, the call for Friday prayer was made at the mosque and people gathered there. There was exceptionally huge number of people. The mosque was filled to end and many had to join the prayer from outside the walls of the mosque compound.

Shortly before the Imam's sermon, an announcement was made by a member of the mosque committee. He spoke of the tragedy across the border and urged both the authorities and the people to stand with the needy people of Darfur in the hour of their need. He asked for donations in cash and kind to help the refugees who crossed the border in droves, and that committees from the people of Tine would be out to locate the gathering points. We received the announcement with great relief and a sense of brotherhood.

After the prayer we approached the members of the committee and asked to coordinate with them. Donations started coming from the traders at the market. There were food items, blankets, plastic mats, bowls and some cash. People also volunteered to distribute the donated items, while others offered their vehicles to transport both the volunteers and the items.

I joined one group and we set out on a very cold evening. We went along the road that runs from Tine to Bahai and met several groups of families in miserable conditions. They stayed either under large trees or in corners of ravine curves. Most of them had almost nothing except the clothing they wore. Few managed to cross with some household belongings. Their children, hungry and cold, were even in worse condition.

The answer to the question of how they were was the same: "Terrible," and on why they fled they answered, "The Janjaweed attacked, killed many of our people, looted our livestock, and burned our villages."

At one point we met a group of five people from the Fur tribe, an old man of about seventy years of age named Owoo Yaaqob, three women - one of whom was about the same age with the elderly man - and a young boy. They had nothing, either by way of mats on the ground or articles used for holding food or water; their feet were bare, made coarse by the cold and walking without shoes.

As we started dropping some food items and mats and blankets for them, one of the women started weeping. The old man explained that they fled their village in Maon in North Jebel Marra on foot as the Janjaweed attacked, firing at people and setting houses on fire. They left behind four very young children who could not run with them and they did not know their fate. At that, almost all the women started weeping. We couldn't lessen their suffering apart from offering words of comfort.

At another location we met a group of elderly men with women and children. When we approached, a tall man introduced himself as Omda Abakar, Chief of Kura Clan of Zaghawa. We dropped some sack of grains for them. The Omda started narrating the calamity which befell his people and the hardship encountered in fleeing and crossing the border with his family, but he was also full of spirit and wanted to fight back by all means.

Before we returned to the town, it was already night and very cold.

CHAPTER SEVENTEEN

$\mathcal{S}$LA/SLM Withdraws From North Darfur

The nights were cold, colder than I have ever experienced in Zaghawa land. The government made good its plan, which was leaked to us long ago, and was on the move on a three-pronged offensive: from Kutum towards Amborow; from Kabkabia towards Kornoye; and from Kulbus towards Tine. On each front we estimated it put three brigades and two or three battalions of Janjaweed militias, with air cover from Antonov bombers and helicopter gun ships.

On the Kutom front, the SLA had Abdalla Shagab commanding some seven to eight hundred fighters, and though out numbered, ill-equipped and ill-armed, they were a highly motivated force and tested in the desert fighting, and could take on any force

On Kabkabia front, the SLA had most of its fine commanders and most of the infantry and artillery since this was the route not only to Kornoye but also to most of Dar Zaghawa vital areas, such as Abgamra, Iditir and the main bases in South Wadi Seyra.

After the wounding of the SLA commander of artillery, Abdelhafi Joma Arabi, and his subsequent evacuation to South Sudan by SPLA for treatment, the SLA deputy commander, Khatir Nano, guarded the southern front.

The government offensive was meant to coincide with the time when SLA commanders and fighters were in their lowest spirits after the death of the chief commander Abdalla Abakar. Every village or settlement on the route of the attacking government forces and Janjaweed militia was burned down,water sources destroyed. As they advanced the population fled a head of them towards the border.

By mid February 2004, the SLA commanders weighed all options open to them. It was clear that the Khartoum regime was out for total war and genocide against the civilian population. A meeting was held in which all options were considered, primarily whether to continue defend the territories held by SLA in north Darfur, or withdraw to the very heart of the government-controlled areas in Central, East and South Darfur.

Logic dictated that there was little benefit defending areas of North Darfur, as the entire population had been completely wiped out either through subjecting them to continous aerial bombardment, thereby making them flee their lands, or through burning down their villages and looting their properties. The alternative was to withdraw deep into Darfur, where the government was in control, but where the SLA could survive, either through contributions from supporters or by seizing from the government forces. The meeting unanimously accepted the idea of withdrawing deep in to Darfur, but deferred the relocation of its high command. Consequently Minni, Joma Hagar, Bakhit Karima and others of SLA remained in Dar Zaghawa. Also remaining in Dar Zaghawa was the whole of SLM or the political wing of the resistance.

Horror and Genocide

I thought I heard a lot about bad things committed by steel-hearted evil human beings against their fellow man. I read about Nero of Rome, Hitler of Germany and the Holocaust, the Rwandan genocide, the killing fields of Bosnia, Pol Pot's regime and the Cambodian mayhems, and even the Omquakias of the Mahdist era in Darfur. I imagined the fear which must have pervaded those lands, but never thought I would be a witness to the one which unfolded in Darfur, precisely at the start of 2004.

Every where there were dead - fields, hills, bushes and ravines. On countless occasions I stumbled on dead bodies especially. Some were mutilated by their killers; others were intact yet decomposed. Many were killed by bullets and machetes. Some just starved in their hiding places.

There were constant earth-shaking sounds of bombs from the air or heavy artillery from the battle fields in Jirjira, Abgamra, Kulbous and the road between Dor and Ambarow. SLA casualties mounted as a result of pitched battles with the Sudanese army for nearly a month in the village of Jirjira.

The dead were abandoned on the battlefields, while the wounded who were lucky enough to be evacuated from the battlefields were in every house in every village from Ain Sirow to Tine and from Kulbus to Mozbed.

The fighters were running out of ammunition, provisions and fuel. Their vehicles were aging and without spare parts. Their captivatingly charismatic and resourceful leader had been killed; divisions were prevalent on all fronts; and morale was low, despite huge efforts from men like Joddo Saqur, Bakhit Karima, and others.

These SLA Commanders penetrated deep into South Darfur for the first time and made a surprising daring raid on Sharia town in January 2004. The SLA made a quick statement to the international media that South Darfur was becoming an SLA- controlled area and that the SLA targets only the Khartoum military.

All hope from across the border was dashed when we were told by the Chadian army general in Tine across the border that his instructions from N'Djamena were not to allow even a single nail to cross the border to Darfur.

People were fleeing the land. Wailing women with retched children in dusty rags fled toward the nearest bushes or hills to hide during the day and try to make a nightly journey to cross the border. Some hopeful ones drove few milk goats; some put their children on donkeys; but the majority tried to get out on foot as fast as possible.

Whole villages were completely deserted. The words, "Arab Janjaweed have entered the land," vibrated across the land, sending fear and terror to all, especially women and children. Terror also came from the air as war planes hovered overhead and dropped bombs on the fleeing women and children.

Their pilots' communication with the Janjaweed and ground forces could be heard even on FM band of the radio. Antonov Captain Mamon told Janjaweed Commander Shukortalla and army Colonel Bashir to let their boys loot the villages and then burn them down. Mamon insisted, "Harik! Harik! Harik! Ya Shukortalla! Ya Bashir!" *To you, Shukortalla and Bashir, burn down! Burn down! Burn down whatever you find"* and tell them *that "General Hamad Nasradin has entered Amborow victorious and found the market quite full. His boys were happy with what they got"!* Mamon told them to not spare any lives for, according to him, we were all Chadian enemies, so we either must be killed or must flee the country.

These were the same people whose women sang for their fighting men to stand firm and brave in front of the Janjaweed Arab enemy, who sought to seize the land.

SLA/SLM Makes Gains Elsewhere

Military wit, raw courage, and environmental and weather conditions - manifested in extraordinary volumes of dust and sand storms - enormously helped the SLA in its planned withdrawal of its main fighting force from extreme far Northwest Darfur to the heart of the enemy territory in Central and Southeast Darfur.

The operation was carried out under the command of the young and taciturn SLA commander Joddo Saqor. It took two weeks to complete. During this period, government warplanes continued their sorties and indiscriminate bombardment of the towns of Kornoye, Tine, Omborow, Mozbed and Idi Tir, as well as the roads leading to them, with huge losses of human lives. Its ground forces advanced without resistance or even sighting meaningful SLA formations in any location.

The government intelligence was fooled into believing that there was no SLA to fight, or that it had either been annihilated or ran across the border to Chad, according to one of their pilots who made a scouting report to his ground commander, as well as the government army and its Janjaweed entering the main towns without resistance.

Based on this, it seemed that Albashir believed his intelligence reports and concluded that he had won the genocidal war against the Darfur resistance. He went to the state controlled national media and declared the crushing of the rebellion and end of military operations in Darfur, a declaration which, after only a few days, turned out to be bogus and ludicrous. The SLA hit hard deep into government controlled areas of Tarne and Tawila in central North Darfur not far from Alfashir, and in Towaisha and Motawarid in eastern North Darfur state.

There was little coordination on the decision of withdrawal between the

SLA sectors in North Darfur and Jebel Marra where Abdulwahid held fort. This was due to difficulty of logistics and the concern SLA commanders in the North had on the reliability of satellite phone communications on the issue. Consequently, the Jebel Marra sector remained in the dark most of the time about the movements of forces in the North.

Because of this, Abdulwahid bought the government side of the story of crushing the rebellion, especially the rumor that government forces entered the strong holds of the SLA in Dar Zaghawa. The later information we heard was that Abdulawahid got in contact with the SPLA leadership and asked for his evacuation from Darfur. The SPLA sent an airplane to Jebel Marra, where Abdulwahid and some of his lieutenants were taken to the South or to Kenya.

In all the SLA operations in Central and East Darfur, the government forces were given bloody nose with heavy losses in men and hardware, especially in the battle of Motawarid which took place around the end of February. Immediately after the battle, the SLA made a statement to the international media which first aired on BBC *Focus on Africa*, declaring that SLA controlled bigger and more economically viable areas than before, and that its operations would spread the width and breadth of the region.

Juddo Saqor and the Emergence of a New Commander

After the death of Abdalla Abakar, the SLA was at a loss. Despite Joma Haqar being an able fighter and not without courage, many within the ranks felt the SLA needed a vibrant and new leadership blood which matched Abakar's qualities. Many commanders of varying abilities were discussed as possible successors, such as Mahamadain Esmail, "Orgajor" Abdalla Shagab and others, until Jodo "Shaqor" surprised many with his exploits and heroic endeavors against the Janjaweed and the Sudanese army.

It was customary among the SLA rank and file that the one with initiative, heroic and leadership qualities always leads. Suddenly, Jodo became a leader despite his young age. Many older commanders rallied around him and a council of commanders accepted him as the SLA Chief of Staff, but in effect he was regarded as the defacto, overall commander, over shadowing Joma Haqar himself, although he had utmost loyalty and respect for Joma.

There were instances when he overruled decisions by Joma and Minni. Even during Abdalla's lifetime, Jodo was revered by Abdalla himself and sought his advice before any decision, but Jodo's exploits were often times viewed by the international observers as contrary to international law. Many foreign observers also speculated that Jodo might become the overall SLA commander in the days ahead.

Unfortunately for the SLA and SLM, a human rights organization gathered bogus information about the role of Jodo in some of the human rights abuses in SLA-controlled areas, especially with government prisoners of war. It is on record that the SLA handed over its prisoners of war to the government side through intermediaries, while the Khartoum regime never produced a single prisoner of war from the movements. The common belief was that the government side executes whomever surrenders. It has special snipers who target the commanders during clashes.

During pitched battles of Jirjira which continued unabated for weeks, the SLM received a call from the Center for Humanitarian Dialogue, HCD- a Geneva-based non-governmental human rights organization, through its director Mr. Andrew Marshal, who in September 2003 visited the SLA in North Darfur. The purpose of the call was that the Center intended, with the help of the international community, to offer the parties an opportunity for a ceasefire and peace talks, and that Mr. Marshal would visit us once again for talks with the SLA and SLM leadership in this respect. We welcomed the Center's offer and expressed readiness to receive Mr. Marshal.

Mr. Marshal called again a week later from N'Djamena informing us that he would arrive at the Tine airstrip in a chartered plane the next morning. I got in touch with Omar Suliman, the SLA Security chief who maintained good relations with the Chadian local authorities in Tine, to inform them of our guest's arrival in Tine and to escort him across the Wadi to our side of Tine.

The next morning Mr. Marshal arrived with a man who looked of Middle Eastern extraction. He was a Sudanese who lived in Switzerland and accompanied Mr. Marshal to translate for him. We took Mr. Marshal across the border to our own Tine and from there to Basawe Valley, where Minni had a temporary camp. Musa Taj eldin of formerly Sudan Federal Democratic Alliance also came with us. On the way we spotted an

Antonov bomber right above us, so we drove under the nearest big tree, a technique we use to avoid detection by the bombers. Mr. Marshal thus had a first hand practical knowledge of our defensive techniques. The bomber passed in the direction of Kornoye.

When we reached Minni, Mr. Marshal spoke on the importance of reaching a ceasefire in Darfur and to allow humanitarian aid to reach the civilians caught up in war. He had the full support of the Americans and the Europeans, as well as the Chadian government on the issue. He went on to say that the Center would make sure that the next round of talks between the Sudan government and the SLA/SLM would be attended by the representatives of the international community. He then requested the support of the SLA/SLM in his efforts.

When he finished talking, we discussed his offer among ourselves and agreed to support him, especially since he gave assurances of the international observance of the talks.

I was delegated to talk to Marshal because I spoke better English than the others. I thanked him and his center first and explained to him that the SLA had no objection to ceasefire, and if it agreed to it, it was not because it was in weak position, but because it was the wish of the international community and because of the dire situation of the civilians - the indiscriminate and constant air bombardment carried out on villages and wells by the government warplanes and attacks by government forces and Janjaweed.

N'Djamena Humanitarian Ceasefire Talks, April 2004

The Chadian government's ambivalence toward the SLA/SLM and its intelligence cooperation with Khartoum contributed much to the encouragement of the Sudanese regime to execute a total war strategy against the SLA/SLM and the communities which produced, harbored and sustained the fighters. The government of Sudan intended to wipe out the communities instead of engaging the SLA in battle, for the battles always ended in its army's defeat and in huge gains to the SLA, both politically and in terms of booty.

To effectively carry out that strategy, it needed more fighting manpower. It also needed groups which were readily willing to do the job with little incentive, groups which were traditionally at loggerheads on resources with the hated communities of Zaghawa, Fur, Massalit and other ethnic groups. Those groups were no other than the Northern Reziqat or Mahamid Arab camel nomads of Northwestern Darfur and some of the Baggaras of South Darfur.

Khartoum could have exterminated every community if it was not for the bold statement put out in March by Mukesh Kapila, the UN humanitarian coordinator for Sudan. He described the situation in Darfur and especially along the border with Chad as "the worst humanitarian disaster in the world" at the time. He also ran a comparison with the Rwandan genocide of 1994 and concluded that the difference was only on scale and numbers killed, and affirmed to the international community that the character of genocide was already in place.

That statement and the security reports on the ground, together with magnitude of the humanitarian situation on the Chad-Sudan border, alarmed both President Idriss Déby and his Chadian government as to the extent the Khartoum government was willing to go to crush the rebellion and, as a result, awaken the international community, especially the U.S. government, which was at the time co-brokering with IGAD the peace talks between the Sudan government and the SPLA/SPLM in Kenya. Déby, who was previously in no mood to mediate between Khartoum and the SLA/SLM,was also under pressure from his own Zaghawa generals,and suddenly had a second thought on the real intentions of Khartoum.

Around the beginning of March, the Khartoum government - after it made certain that no civilians remained in North Darfur, especially around the towns of Dor, Ombarow, Mozbed, Kornoye, Foraweya, and Tine, which were either partially burned down or destroyed by aerial bombardment - announced that President Albashir would visit Alfashir to show the international community that he had crushed the rebellion and that he controls Darfur.

SLA quickly put up a statement declaring that if Albashir came to Darfur, he would be a target of SLA forces. The statement was broadcast on the radio program *Voice of Sudan of NDA*, which was then aired from Eritrea. The government took the statement seriously and Albashir's visit was cancelled.

The following day I had a call from the British Embassy and an official named Mark informed me that a group of European Union diplomats from Britain, the Netherlands, Germany, France, Italy, Greece, and the EU Commission representative in Sudan were coming to Alfashir. On their itinerary was a meeting with SLA/SLM leadership.

Mark said that from Alfashir the group intended to travel by a helicopter provided by the UN military commission in the Nuba Mountains to an SLA-controlled area to meet with Minni and others, probably in Mozbed or any where around Mozbed which was convenient to SLA leaders, and that he needed coordinates for the location where their helicopter would land.

I had my reservations on possibility of such meeting taking place between us and such high powered delegation from the EU. I also reflected on the logic that such number of ambassadors should risk their lives to come to SLA controlled areas in a helicopter, but in any case, I got in touch with Minni and informed him of the request along with my reservations. Although Minni was also skeptical, he agreed with me to forward the coordinates to Mark.

On the appointed date and time, which also was very windy, Minni moved to the area, although not to the specific spot. The government bombers, as if they were instructed by Khartoum to sabotage the effort, intensified their bombardment around the same area, making it impossible for the visit to take place, and I believe it was cancelled due to fake government reports on the security situation in the area.

On March 14th, 2004, I had a call from Minni telling me that he had calls from Ms. Janice Elmore at the American Embassy and Mark of the British Embassy. They discussed with him the possibility of a ceasefire on humanitarian grounds. He also said I should expect calls from the two on the possibility of going to N'Djamena for talks with government delegation. He also added that he had calls from both Mr. Roger Winter, a U.S. State Department envoy to Sudan, and our friend Andrew Marshal, suggesting the same idea of humanitarian ceasefire talks and possibly an agreement with the government.

The next day I took the initiative and a called Mrs. Elmore. She answered the call with a deep and very attentive voice. She went straight to the point and asked what were our concerns and terms of going to Chad.

I was both surprised that the American Embassy cared about our security concerns and encouraged by her understanding of our situation.

I told her that we accepted the ceasefire proposal purely on humanitarian grounds, for the sake of our people on the ground who were constantly subjected to attacks and aerial bombardment, and because the international community want it. However, we needed security guarantees within the Chadian territory and while entering and exiting that country, and that the SLM/SLA wanted the international community – the UN, AU, EU, US and the neighboring countries - to be represented at the talks. She took note of that and assured me that the security of our delegation would be guaranteed.

After our conversation, I had a call from Omar Suliman, the SLA's Chief of Security, as Minni also informed him about his contacts with the Americans, and the arrangements being made to go to N'Djamena. I informed both Minni and Omar the details of my discussions with the American Embassy official and the security guarantees she promised in Chad.

Three days later, a delegation for the talks was selected from field commanders and some politicians in SLA controlled areas. They included:

Minni Minnawi as head of the SLA/SLM
Omar Suliman
Adam Shugar
Mohammed Morsal
Bakhit Hamid
Bahar Arabie
Suliman Marjan
Abdu Abdalla (Bergi)
Soqor Krinik
Adam Alnor

Faisal Salih (Minni's aide-de-camp and head of his security detail).
Also included was Jibril Teck, the commander of the then little-known Justice and Equality Movement (JEM) of Khalil Ibrahim, who was in dispute with his movement's chief and defected.

Other commanders were also selected from the SLA/SLM Western Darfur sector commanded by Khamis Abakar. They included:

> Yusif Ahmed Hamid
> Ali Hamid
> Jamal Arbab
> Monsor Arbab

The SLA/SLM delegation from the field was to be joined by others from outside Darfur, including the SLA/SLM chairman Abdulwahid Nor, who was coming from Nairobi with Ahmed Abdelshafi. Others were:

> Dr. Sharif Harir from Norway
> Abdalla Domi, who had left for Dubai before the SLA withdrawal
>   from North Darfur, also came with Mobarak Nahar from
>   Dubai
> Nahar Authman Nahar from the Netherlands

Both the U.S. government and the international community insisted, despite the Chadian government's reluctance, that the Justice and Equality Movement (JEM) of Khalil Ibrahim, which was fighting beside the SLA but controlled little or no territories, should also be brought to the talks, thereby according recognition for the first time to the JEM.

The reluctance of the Chad government on the inclusion of the JEM into the talks was born out of the belief that the movement was an arm of the Popular Congress party, which was at loggerheads with the ruling National Congress Party. It was viewed as an Islamist movement, particularly because it was headed by Khalil Ibrahim, the former die-hard National Islamic Front member and a prominent Jihadist in the South Sudan war on behalf of Khartoum's Islamic government, and included in its ranks well-known Islamists.

The small JEM delegation which came from the field was headed by the energetic Abubakar Hamid and Mohammad Salih Haraba, while a much larger delegation of highly educated persons came from Europe.

On the appointed day we moved to the border town of Bahai and crossed to the Chadian side with our vehicles to the air strip. We met a military-type transport plane. Beside the plane were Mr. Roger Winter, the French ambassador to Chad who spoke some Arabic, and our friend Mr. Andrew Marshal of the Center for Humanitarian Dialogue. It was obvious that Mr. Winter was both surprised and excited at the sight of our vehicles. Little time was spent on exchange of greetings and we boarded the plane for N'Djamena.

On arrival, Chadian security agents insisted that we must be searched for weapons, but I vehemently resisted their demand and a wild drama ensued. Eventually, the Chadian security agents agreed we could proceed to the town without being searched.

The talks between our delegation and the JEM delegation on one side and the Sudan government delegation on the other side were officially declared opened on March 16th, 2004, by the Chadian foreign affairs minister. The international community was fully represented as we demanded. I made the opening remarks of our delegation while Minni delivered the key address. When Mr. Winter wanted to make a statement on behalf of the US government, the Sudan government delegation withdrew, making Mr. Winter decline to make his remarks.

The actual negotiations started the following day, preceded by consultations. President Déby sent word through the organizers of the talks that he wanted to meet with four leaders of the SLM/SLA. Our delegation decided that Abdulwahid, Minni Minnawi, Dr. Harir and I should go to the meeting with the president.

The president reiterated the appeal of ending the war for the sake of the suffering population of Darfur, and that he would do everything possible to achieve peace. He spoke for about thirty minutes, and then paused to hear from us. We took turns explaining our position. I explained that the war was imposed on us and on the people of Darfur by the Arabist Islamist regime in Khartoum, and that the regime carried out genocide using Arab tribes of the region, including Chadian Arabs. The president listen with attention, then said, "Any government, if faced by a rebellion, would use whatever means available to crush it."

As the talks entered the second day, President Déby decided to chair the talks. He was assisted by a representative from the African Union Commission, a Mr. Sam Ibok. The president proved to be a master mediator and excellent negotiator. Our side appointed Dr. Harir to be the chief negotiator, while the JEM side appointed Ahmed Togod as their chief negotiator. For the next several days and nights of the talks, Dr. Harir did a brilliant job, most often speaking for both movements. He eclipsed all other speakers at the talks so that the government chief negotiator seemed intimidated by Harir's intellectual verbosity.

On April 4th, the Humanitarian Ceasefire Agreement was reached and signed. Minni singed on behalf of the SLA/SLM. A problem brewed on the JEM side as to who must sign the document on behalf of the movement. While Khalil delegated to Harba and another member to sign the document, Jibril Tik declared that he was the legitimate commander of the JEM; therefore he was the one who was supposed to sign.

The delegates waited for about three days to resolve the issue, but rumors started to spread that Jibril Tik was selling out to the Sudan government or that he had been paid to create the problem. Eventually three people signed on behalf of the JEM.

The agreement provided for the establishment of a joint ceasefire commission under the African Union, comprising parties to the talks and Chad and the African Union. Modalities and mechanisms of implementation were laid out accordingly. Our side appointed Adam Shugar as representative, to be assisted by Jamal Adam, Abdu Bergi, and Mansur Arabab. The latter abandoned the assignment after a while for reasons best known to him and left Chad for Asmara to join Abdulwahid.

Shugar remained in the assignment until mid or late 2005 when he also had a change of heart about the SLM/SLA leadership, especially about being subordinate to Minni Minnawi. He opted to act as his own movement's leader, creating a small following from his own extended family. He remained in N'Djamena for the duration of the ceasefire, boycotting both the Abuja talks and other SLA/SLM functions, up to the signing of Abuja Peace Agreement of May 2006, when afterward he decided to defect and join the Justice and Equality Movement

Immediately after the talks, travel arrangements were hurriedly made for us and we departed the following day for Darfur, accompanied by officials from the American Embassy in Chad.

With the International Media & NGOs, April-August 2004

On arrival to Darfur from N'Djamena, we were received by an SLA force of several vehicles led by commanders Abdalla Shaghab, Mohammad Sholla, Mohammadian Orgajor, Khatir Shatta, Jabir Eshaq and others. We spent the night together on the outskirts of Wadi Hawar. Early in the morning, the force dispersed to different directions. Myself, Khatir Shatta, Omar Suliman and Yusif Ahmed Hamid became one group.

Beside my role of spokesman, I was also assigned the role of coordinator for the international media and the non-governmental organizations which sought to enter Darfur to document the atrocities. My role required I should be stationed at the border between Sudan and Chad to help the internationals who were denied entry to Darfur by Khartoum authorities to enter and move freely under the protection of the SLA/SLM.

Among those I have escorted were correspondents from the BBC, CNN, *Washington Post*, the AP, French television, and other journalists from Norway, the Netherlands, the Republic of Ireland, and Italy. Prominent among these was Christian Amanpour of the CNN. I have also escorted fact-finding officials from the Human Rights Watch.

In the course of my work as NGO's coordinator, I managed to visit the refugee camps on the Chad side of the border. My visit to the Eridimi camps in May 2004 coincided with the visit by the Secretary General of United Nations, Mr. Kofi Anan. At the time my family was also part of the refugees. They lived through all the harsh conditions which the survivors of the genocide passed through.

At Eridimi, as in all other camps, people lived in squalid conditions, with whole family households sleeping and living in one small tent. There was no privacy whatsoever for anyone, and the sanitary conditions were horrible.

People used holes dug in the ground as toilets, or took to the bush to relieve themselves. This led to the spread of many diseases like diarrhea, especially among young children. The child mortality rate also increased due to malnutrition and lack of proper medical care.

Despite the initial sympathy and help from the local Chadian population, the relationship between the refugees and the locals soon turned into rivalry over the meager resources. Some locals began to mistreat the new comers and prevented them from doing things like gathering fire wood from the bushes near farm lands, drawing water from the locals wells, or herding on the land. There were instances that the refugees were either molested or abused and insulted, but the Chadian authorities were exemplery in their dealing with the refugee population. The United Nations High Commision For Refugees did a great job in providing water at the camp sites, thereby reducing the friction between the two sides.

On occasion I held, with the help of Yusif Ahmed Hamid, meetings with the refugee leaders to counsel them and to brief them about the peace efforts being made by the Chad government and the international community.

I was in and out of these camps until I was called to attend the first Abuja peace talks in August 2004.

The First Abuja Peace Talks, August-September 2004

Sharif Harir starred in the N'Djamena Humanitarian Ceasefire talks, and when the first Abuja Inter-Sudanese peace talks on Darfur opened, he was an old hand in the art of negotiation with government side, only that in Abuja, both the mediation and the format were different.

While in N'Djamena, the Chad government with its limited resources was in control of the talks, but in Abuja the African Union took charge, and the delegates were afforded all the best facilities obtainable in Africa.

At the start of first Abuja peace talks, it was apparent that differences between Abdulwahid and Minni would bear heavily on the talks. Abdulwahid had lost full control of the movement by his departure from the field in Darfur at the start of government offensive of January 2004. He had also lost a great deal of military respect, especially in North Darfur, and Minni naturally moved in to fill the vacuum.

Since the N'Djamena Humanitarian Ceasefire Agreement - signed by Minni on behalf of the movement, although Abdulwahid was present and without recourse to Abdulwahid or authorization - Abdulwahid was making efforts to gain authority. One of those efforts was his opposition to the signing of the agreement without a convincing reason. It was apparent that he believed Minni in his absence might delegate someone else, probably Dr. Harir the chief negotiator, to sign the agreement and not Abdulwahid.

He swayed several members of the delegation to accept his position, despite my attempts to let the agreement through and despite efforts by Mr. Hamid Alqabid, then AU mediator on Darfur, and President Olusegun Obasanjo, who called for a meeting with a two-member delegation from each of the SLM and JEM movements to discuss the issue.

Dr. Harir and I went to the meeting with President Obasanjo with the JEM delegation, comprising Ahmed Togod and Ahmed Hissein. After many security checks at the gates of the Nigerian state house, we were let into the Agoda presidential villa. After about ten minutes, the president came in. He was in light Nigerian garment made of Guinea brocade with a matching Yoruba cap. He greeted us with warm handshakes and immediately launched into the reason behind his invitation. It was clear that he had little background information as to what led to the conflict in Darfur and the tactics used by Albashir's government to end the conflict, which resulted in indiscriminate attacks on both the civilians and the rebels.

We made a full explanation of the root causes of the conflict and the demands of the movements, which were essentially equitable power sharing and wealth sharing. When we mentioned the issue of wealth sharing, the president seemed bemused and asked jokingly, "Is there any wealth in Sudan, or for that matter, in Africa in general?" then added, "I thought wealth is only in America."

He urged us to soften our positions and offer compromises, and said he would also speak with the government side. We promised him to be as flexible as possible.

Back at the hotel, we held several meetings to resolve the issue with Abdulwahid but without success. As differences became sharp between those who supported Abdulwahid's position and those who agreed to the signing of the agreement, Dr. Harir suggested a vote on the matter. In the end, Abdulwahid's position became the meeting's majority position.

CHAPTER EIGHTEEN

$\mathcal{D}$ivisions in the Darfur Movements

On September 23rd, 2005, approximately a week from the end of the first Abuja talks,Minni called informing me that a Sudan donors' conference was coming up in about three day's time in Oslo, the Norwegian capital, and that the SLM was invited to attend the conference. The selection was made for Dr. Sharif Harir, Ahmed Abdelshafi and me to represent the movement. It was a rather short notice, but at the same time it was an event which the SLM must be represented at since it was invited,and it was an international gathering.

I made quick arrengments and travelled down to Abuja to get my visa and ticket to Norway. I had little wait at the Norwagian Embassy,the staff was very cordial. The tickect was provided through our old friend Mr Marshal's CHD,and I travelled through London to Oslo. I attended the meeting with Dr. Harir and Ahmed Abdelshafi. It was an august gathering that brought the Sudanese waring parties and dignitaries from many international organizationsand the USA,EU,AU and the UN. The Norwagian minister for international development opened the meeting with remarks that were both encouraging and uplifting to the Sudanese. On the SLM side, there was no clear indication as to who must be the leader of our delegation, but at the venue and immediately before the meetings started we agreed that Dr. Harir should lead us and he delivered the remarks of our delegation.

After the conference I seized the opportunity to tour Oslo and also visited the Harir family at their beautiful home at the outskirts of Oslo, where I met his wife Ann Magrid and his son Elyas.

The Second Abuja Peace Talks and the Humanitarian Security Enhancement Agreement, November 2004

The second round of talks in Abuja started in November 2004 and dragged on for about three weeks. The government side, represented by Mahjzoob Alkhalifa, adopted a harder line. At the same time, the government offensive on the ground in Darfur increased, with more villages being burned and thousands displaced in East and Central Darfur.

Meanwhile, the differences among the movements - whether or not to sign the Humanitarian Security Enhancement Agreement - lingered on. Abdulwahid did not want to sign the agreement. The movement also staged a two day boycott of the talks, demanding the government stop its offensives. I also made a statement to the international media on behalf of the two movements.

Toward the third week into the talks, Minni Minnawi, who hitherto was not at the talks, arrived from Asmara. The international community persuaded him to sign the agreement, thereby ending the problem. Strangely enough, Abdulwahid did not object to Minni's decision to sign.

With the signing of the Humanitarian Security Enhancement, the talks were adjourned and the AU mission in Darfur was given the mandate to offer greater monitoring of the N'Djamena ceasefire and protection of civilians.

Divisions

The cracks within the SLM were becoming apparent and worrying not only to those who loved Darfur and its revolution, but also to the AU and the international community at large, especially the U.S. government which tried so hard to end the conflict in the South and wanted a united front at minimum within the Darfur movements to end the conflict there.

The most worry symptom within the SLM was the appearance of tribal trends. The SLM was beginning to polarize along tribal lines. This started with statements attributed to Abdulwahid, when he claimed that at the formation of the movement in Jebel Marra, the founding members assigned the chairmanship to a Fur, the vice chairmanship to a Massalit, and the commander general to a Zaghawa. Such a statement was refuted by others who first formed the movement and its army and pushed the people to stick to the purported formula. Others who did not belong to the three mentioned groups became alienated and began to look for ways to accommodate them.

Minni Minnawi also resented the statement; thus began a rivalry between him and Abdulwahid. Abdulwahid named Khamis Abakar, head of Darmasalit sector of the SLA, as his deputy, replacing the earlier appointment of Mansor Arbab. It was apparent that this decision was taken unilaterally, at a time when Abdulwahid was not in the field and controlled little of the SLA /SLM on the ground.

This decision put Minni on the defensive; an intense dislike developed between the two men with ominious consequences on the movement. Their differences had nothing to do with the cause, for which both fought to achieve. They were hated or even marked for elimination by the Khartoum regime because of their work. It was personal and immature, purely on issues of prominence within the movement. Both men were obsessed with a leadership complex and viewed any desenting voice as a potential enemy and a coup plotter.

Attempts at reconciliation were made by some of the preeminent members of the movement and by the Eritrean government, but to no avail. Soon, some members of the international community became worried because of their rivalry.

As part of the international community's concern on the future of the SLM, the Italian non-governmental organization known as Sainta Egidio organized, with the support of U.S. State Department, a workshop for the SLM and JEM leadership in Rome. The workshop was well attended, although key personalities including Minni, Dr. Harir and Khalil Ibrahim refused to come. The conference was intended to bring the individual SLM and the relatively small JEM leadership members closer and create a unified front to negotiate with the government of Sudan for the good of the Darfur cause.

The Italian government was not present at any stage of the workshop, but the U.S. State Department was represented by the staff of its Sudan programs group. It was also the first time the delegates of the two movements became acquainted with Ambassador John Yates, who was newly appointed as the U.S. representative for Inter-Sudanese peace talks on Darfur. Mr. Yates was a reserved but friendly man who made friends with many of us.

The workshop achieved little by way of closing the differences or bringing together the divergent views of the perceived Abdelwahid supporters and Minni supporters. Instead, a bad relationship developed between Abdulwahid and Abdeljabar Dosa, who was warming up to take the role of chief negotiator in case Dr. Harir was absent.

When the next round of talks started, Mr. Yates was a familiar face to many of us. He and Ms. Janice Elmore played a vital role in ensuring the talks continued with all smoothness and without acrimony, until it culminated in the declaration of principles.

The movements also lost their dear friend during the conclusion of third round of talks in the person of Janice Almore, who fell ill with malaria and withdrew from the U.S. team. Janice always advised the movements for moderation and to think of the plight of the people on the ground in the IDP and refugee camps, but she was also firm supporter of the rights of the people and justice in Sudan.

Her role was filled with an equally able and energetic lady and friend in the person of Kathleen Fitzgibbon, the political officer at the US embassy in Chad.

Dr. Harir Withdraws

On the field in Darfur, the government was taking every opportunity to empty the SLM/SLA controlled areas of its population and wipe out the movements. Its ground and air offensives increased day and night while at the same time the AU and the international community were busy and keen to find a peaceful resolution to the crisis.

In one of these offensives, the energetic leader Abdalla Domi was wounded. The movement managed to evacuate him to Chad, from where he was taken to Dubai and within few months gained full recovery. After that, Domi returned to Darfur only to be ambushed by JEM fighters in the town of Mahajiria and killed.

The circumstances which led to his death, as depicted by eye witnesses, were that around June 2005 the SLA/SLM was in control of the town of Mahajiria - traditionally a Birgid tribal area - which the SLA dislodged from government forces a few months prior. A small force of JEM fighters were also in town. They were there as fellow comrades in the struggle. The chief of Birgid sent word from Neyala (where he took refuge at the time of fighting between SLA and government forces) that he intended to return to Mahajiria and that he needed his home, which was at the time occupied by the JEM force.

Domi, with all the characteristics of good intentions known of him, went to the JEM base and demanded the JEM commander and his men relocate to another empty house in town. He was dragged into an argument and eventually fired upon. He died instantly.

After this incident, the SLA units in Mahajiria and East Darfur retaliated, attacking JEM positions in all East Darfur. In the process, JEM lost a lot in terms of men and material. Domi's death also cast a heavy shadow on the future of the SLM, very similar to the death of Abdalla Abakar in the previous year. It also affected Dr. Harir's chances of fully incorporating within SLM/SLA, as Domi was one of his staunchest allies and sought to consolidate him within the resistance movement.

At the start of the third round of the Abuja talks, Dr. Harir, who made an impact on all the delegates, declined to appear. Aside from the death of his chief ally Domi, nobody knows what made him withdraw from the Abuja talks. Some news that we had about him were that he was sick and admitted in to a hospital. His withdrawal was not a good decision either for him, for the movements, and the Darfur cause in general. Despite the position he held within our movement, he was needed in Abuja for the sake of the cause and for the sake of his own political future. His withdrawal left a vacuum of an adept negotiator not only for the SLM but for the whole of our side of the table. With his departure, the movements lost an articulate voice, respected by the AU mediation and the international community, and hated by the government side.

We did our best to fill the gap. There were a number of potential successors to the role, such as Abakar Abulbashar, Abdeljabar Dosa and Bahar Arabie. Minni and his group in Asmara sent Abdeljabar Dosa to be the chief negotiator. Though Dosa was an articulate Arabic speaker and able negotiator, he lacked some of Harir's competencies. One of the things which made Harir a prominent negotiator was his scholarly fluency in English and the distinct and coherent manner he expressed our position, a thing which always made our position very clear to the mediation and the observers from the international community. He gave more confidence to our negotiating team as to our ability to deal with the highly trained government side led by the cunning and arrogant Majzoob Al-Khalifa.

Instead of considering Harir's competencies and capabilities and allow him to be in a lead position, he was viewed by many within our group as someone trying to take over the leadership of the movement. This, in addition to the position adopted by some of his supporters in his own former SFDA who viewed his efforts in Abuja as being exploited by Abdulwahid and Minni for their own personal political gains,this made him decline farther participation in the talks. His disappearance from the talks was the defining moment of the beginning of his political decline.

The Fourth Round of Talks and the Declaration of Principles

The fourth round of the Abuja Peace talks started in May and continued through June 2005. This was some months after our workshop in Rome. The SLM/A was still one strong united movement, despite the difficult times we all had with each other, especially between Abdulwahid and Minni and the cracks which appeared from time to time due to acrimonious debates and graspy arguments, mainly between what was perceived as Abdulwahid's group and Minni's group.

This round was also the most heavily attended by the representatives of the international community. For the first time, Eritrea was represented by one of the influential ruling party officials, Abdalla Jabir, who had good relations with the SLM, especially with Minni Minnawi.

In addition to its ambassador in Chad who used to attend all meetings, Libya sent two more officials: a top security official named Ali Ben Nasir and a director in its foreign service. The representatives of the other members of the international community included Chadians, Americans, British, French, Norwegians, the UN, and the Arab League.

On the movement's side we had a rather huge delegation, especially the SLM, because the differences and mistrust between Abdulwahid and Minni reached a point that they could not agree on a list of delegates to attend the talks.

This was also the time Abdelwahid declared the expulsion of five prominent members of the movement on grounds best known to him, but the stated reason was that the five were anti-peace. These included the spokesman Mahjub Hissein, Adam Alnur, Abdelaziz Sam, Ali Trayo, and Bahar Arabie. All were also perceived by him as Minni supporters. The declaration had little effect, as he himself knew that he lacked any means of enforcing it.

Judging from the role assigned to me on the list in the talks, it was apparent that either Minni or someone who helped him prepare the list had some issues with me. Despite being a pioneer of these talks and my vast experience in the dynamics of the conflict, I was not assigned any significant role that could put me in a front position at the negotiating table.

Instead, new faces which had nothing or very little to do with the actual struggle were put in leading roles, both by Abdulwahid and Minni, simply because it was tribally expedient to have them a long,or they held higher university degrees. People like Dr Abdelrahaman Musa, Ibrahim Madibo, Dr Eltijani Bodor and others from places like Canada, Europe and the Gulf were put in charge of commissions and committees. These were people who knew nothing of the reality on the ground or whole heartedly believed in the objectives of the movement,they had no supporters whatsoever in rank and file of the movement. They were simply job or prominence seekers.

Nevertheless, I did not show any resentment and accepted the arrangement of the group in Asmara in a positive mood. I thought if these new people could fight on the negotiating table and achieve results, so be it. At the same time I volunteered to be the link between the representatives of the international community and my group, and on this I developed good working relations with the American delegation, which was the most active and most concerned about the direction of the talks.

Anticipating the continuation of the negotiation to a final agreement, the heads of the negotiating commissions were named with Abdeljabar Dosa as chief negotiator. As the AU pushed ahead with the talks, it became clear the differences between the two groups were marring the progress of the talks. Most of the differences appeared when Abdulwahid was in attendance of a meeting and people divided along Fur group and Zaghawa group, or Abdulwahid's group and the perceived Minni's group.

At one point, Abdulwahid's began to classify certain members of the international community as supporters of Minni's group, especially Chad. When the JEM, which had bad relations with the Chadian government, tried to exclude Chad from the joint mediation, a thing which they could only do with the support of the SLM, Abdulwahid agreed with them and sent a joint note to the AU requesting Chad's withdrawal from the co-mediation in the name of the SLM and without consulting with the rest of the delegation. Abdulwahid even went further and joined the JEM delegation to meet President Obasanjo to demand the withdrawal of Chad.

On this, the AU chief negotiator Mr. Sam Ibok hurriedly convened a plenary meeting to discuss the letter and read it out loud, at which point the representatives of Chad, Ahmed Alam and Mohammad Ali Abdalla, immediately left the room. We were caught unaware and requested more time to discuss the matter within the movement and the meeting was adjourned on that basis. We hurriedly held our meeting with Abdulwahid in attendance, which turned out to be one of the rowdiest. Most of the perceived Minni team did not attend.

I personally confronted Abdulwahid with several facts and the reality on the ground, especially the role Chad played since the beginning of the struggle in Darfur and the many of our refugees it hosted on its land, and that Chad had interest in Darfur because what affected Darfur affected Chad, too. If the SLM wanted to solve the problem without Chad's involvement, it would be a difficult task.

Omar Suliman spoke in the same vein with an even louder voice. Our speeches had an impact on the rest of the group, who first and foremost blamed Abdulwahid for taking a unilateral decision to send the note to AU, then emphasized on the role of Chad in the resolution of the problem.

Abdulwahid tried to justify his position but he was overwhelmed by dissent. Eventually he agreed to retract the request for Chad's withdrawal. Abdelrahaman Musa, as head of the delegation's information committee, and some one who also spoke French, was delegated to deliver the SLM retraction in French in a plenary to impress upon the now seriously alienated Chadian delegation. We requested for the plenary and the mediation agreed.

After Musa delivered the SLM written position and handed it to the mediation and the Chad delegation moved from the observer seat to the co-mediation seat, Ahmed Abdelshafi, a senior member of the perceived Abdulwahid group, made an intervention which surprised the meeting. He declared that the SLM position contained in the chairman's letter to the mediation remained as it was, but the mediation ignored his statement.

The talks, with their aim to agree on principles of negotiations, dragged on for weeks without any sign either party was willing to give way. The government side objected to almost every proposal the movements presented. The movements, too, adopted a hard line stance in the beginning and insisted that issues such as self-determination for Darfur should be included in the principles.

President Obasanju, as host government and head of the African Union, intervened on more than one occasion but without success. The AU mediation became weary and was on the verge of adjourning the talks.

Suddenly, the Libyan foreign minister Ali Triki arrived Abuja on a surprise visit and came directly to the venue of the talks, lodging at the same hotel. That evening he made a dramatic statement on an Aljazira TV station declaring that the movements had accepted to sign the declaration of priniciples. Mahjub Hissein, the now SLM spokesman at large, made a counter statement on the same Aljazira TV station at the same time Altriki was making his statement and denied that any such agreement had been reached. Why or on what Altriki based his statement, no one could tell. One interpretation was that he believed that the movements were politically naïve and no one among them could reject a conclusion by him.

At this point I had a call one very early morning from the U.S. representative at the talks, Ambassador John Yates, where he expressed his deep concern at the lack of progress on the talks and urged me to get a select group of wise men from our side, including Abdulwahid, to meet with him immediately at his room in the same hotel we were.

At same time he reached for Abdulwahid to attend the meeting, I did my best to get as many level-headed delegates as possible. They included Abdeljabar Dosa, Ali Trayo, Ahmed Abdelshafi, Omar Suliman, and

Dr. Salah Mana. Abdulwahid also got Abdelrahaman Musa, Nusradin, Abulgasim Imam, and Khamis Abakar.

We converged in Mr. Yates' room. The ambassador spoke for about ten minutes, expressing the U.S. State Department's concern and his personal concern on the lack of progress. The issue of the principles was not an agreement he stated. It was simply a declaration. Mr. Yates encouraged us to give it a serious consideration because signing it would not jeopardize any of our negotiating positions.

I also spoke in support of the ambassador and urged my colleagues to sign the proposal presented by AU mediation. The rest of the delegates accepted the idea and we agreed with Mr. Yates that he could inform the AU and the international facilitators about this breaking news.

The AU did not waste time and immediately called for a plenary session, where the announcement was made. In the evening, a signing ceremony was held. Khamis Abakar, as deputy head of the movement, signed on behalf of the movement.

At Tripoli, July 2005

Immediately after the signing of the declaration of principles, we had word from Ali Ben Nasir, the Libyan representative, that Colonel Gaddafi or the Libyan government wanted to see our delegation in Tripoli to congratulate us for signing of the declaration of principles. According to him, it was an important milestone and the visit would afford us a convenient venue for retreat to reflect and mend the cracks within the organization. Ben Nasir informed us that a Libyan plane would be in Abuja to convey us.

The flight to Tripoli took about three and a half hours, during which we ate a lavish meal. Some had alcoholic drinks which made them inebriated and resulted in arguments on issues which had nothing to do with our mission to Tripoli.

On arrival to Tripoli, we were taken to Al–Mehari Hotel, a luxurious five-star hotel where the Libyan government hosts its guests. Each was allocated a standard room, and for the next four weeks we were given kid glove treatment. We were provided with free food and drink, free laundry and free entertainment.

It was a wonderful opportunity both for the leaders of the two movements, Abdulwahid, Khalil, Khamis, Minni and the other members to cement relationships and forge greater unity, but instead precious time was wasted discussing what differed us instead of what united us and the people of Darfur.

The Tripoli visit also came against the backdrop of clashes in the field, between SLA forces and fighters loyal to the JEM, where Abdalla Domi, the respected SLA/SLM commander, was murdered in Mahajiria. For me and many within the SLA/SLM, the loss of Domi was a huge blow to our struggle. He had been a dynamo which moved the organization and an animator of things. The Libyan government proposed an end of hostilities,between SLA and JEM fighters,and was accepted by Minni and Khalil,accordingly an agreement was signed.

One of the major issues which consumed our time and energy in Al-Mehari hotel was when and where we were going to have the SLM general conference. While Minni and many of us echoed what the commanders on the ground wanted, Abdulwahid, supported by Khamis, had a different opinion. The commanders wanted the conference to be held in SLA/SLM controlled areas, but Abdulwahid want it held in the Libyan border town of Alkofra. Committees which formed to discuss the issue were divided along pro-field and pro-Alkofra lines.

Eventually we had a whole house meeting – and it was a rowdy one. For the first time I witness Abdulwahid and Minni vent against each other, though they stopped short of name calling and a declaration of animosity against each other. It was obvious their quarrel would have ominous consequences on the whole movement and on the Darfur struggle.

During the Tripoli visit, a select group of the movement's members which included Minni but excluded Abdulwahid were summoned by the Libyan intelligence chief, Abdella Sanusi, where Mr. Sanusi directly accused me and Mahjub Hissein of working against the efforts of achieving peace in Darfur. He stopped short of threatening us. It was concerning to get such a warning from a man known for his ruthlessness. Both Mahjub and myself defended our positions vehemently.

At the end of the meeting, Mr. Sanusi proposed the two of us meet in Tripoli the Khartoum government intelligence chief the notorious Salah Gosh as soon as possible to strike a deal on behalf of the movement.

Initially we showed no objection to the proposal, but believing that such a clandestine deal with a regime that has all the Darfuri blood in its hands would work counter to the objective of the movement and the interests of the people of Darfur, we played tactics to frustrate it.

CHAPTER NINETEEN

$\mathcal{N}$'Djamena – The Organizing Committee, September 2005

On August 30th, 2005, after one month in Tripoli, the movement had polarized more and almost became two factions - one supporting Abdulwahid and the other supporting Minni. We then received an unofficial invitation from the Chadian government to visit Nd'jamena. It seemed diplomatic rivalry was going on between the countries of the region, each trying to have greater influence on the issue of Darfur and on the movements, especially the SLM.

While Abdulwahid showed a lack of interest in the Chad visit and instead prepared to leave for Kenya, our group accepted the invitation. Two delegations were formed for visits to Chad and Eritrea to brief their governments on the declaration of the principles agreement and the situation on the ground. We decided that while Minni and others would head to the field in Darfur to prepare for the conference, Abdeljabar Dosa, Abdelaziz Sam, Mohammad Tijani and others would head for Asmara. On Chad's delegation was myself, Adam Elnor, Mahjub Hissein, Mohammad Harin, and Ali Trayo, and I was supposed to be the head of the delegation.

Dosa was not content with going to Asmara and showed displeasure. He even indicated that he lost interest in the movement and wanted to return to his family in Saudi Arabia. At this point, Minni suggested he could head the Chad delegation, a suggestion he happily accepted.

We departed Tripoli at the beginning of August on an Air Afriqiyah flight to N'Djamena via Kano in Nigeria. The following morning we were visited by many of our compatriots and emissaries from Dawsa Déby, the president's half brother who was also in charge of the Darfur file.

Dawsa invited us to lunch with him in his house, where we were delighted to meet our old friends Ahmed Alam and Mohammad Ali Abdalla, Chad's representatives at the Inter-Sudanese peace talks in Abuja.

Dawsa also brought up the issue of Dr. Sharif Harir and Adam Shugar, who had gone to the Darfur border area from N'Djamena with followers, cash and weaponery (albeit on the other side of the border) but were stopped from entering either by the commander in charge of the area, or by Minni, on the basis that their intentions were not clear,more specially some members of their group had earlier made a declaration of overthrowing the leadership of the movement. In Dawsa's view, Harir and Shugar were core SLM/SLA and should not be stopped from entering the field. We expressed to Dawsa our regret that this happened and that we as a delegation are willing to meet them to discuss the matter to resolve it.

Two days later, arrangements were made by Dawsa's office to be received by President Déby in the presidential villa. We sat down as a delegation and discussed how our meeting with the president would be and agreed on points to be made by Abdeljabar Dosa as head of the delegation. We were accompanied on the president's visit by Dawsa himself and a certain Feki Bedradin,a religious man with gotee beard and a Saudi style head cover, whose role was not clear, but was said to be a religious councelor and have easy access to the president.

When we met the president, he was his usual self though was not in high spirits. Dawsa made the introduction to our delegation, beginning with Abdeljabar Dosa, and when he began my introduction he reminded the president of the role I played in 1989-1990 in Nigeria in support of the MPS, the president's then rebel movement organization. The president though seemed attentive to what Dosa Debi said but did not underline the part about my role with MPS.

Abdeljabar Dosa briefed the president on our mission. He spoke in fairly good diplomatic language, thanking the president for receiving us in such a short notice despite his busy schedule, then explained the situation on the ground in Darfur and the SLM's position on the peace talks and the declaration of principles it signed with the government of Sudan. He explained the internal difficulties the movement was passing through and that plans were made for a general conference to resolve them and have a new institutional structure which would accommodate all.

Abdeljabar Dosa stressed how Chad's assistance was needed along with the rest of the international community. In conclusion, he spoke about the situation where Dr. Harir and Adam Shugar – who by now became undeclared defectors - were stopped by SLA command from crossing to Darfur. He also expressed our sincere desire to open dialogue with them and reach an amicable agreement, whereby they would honorably return to their rightful position within the SLM fold and participate in the arrangements of restructuring the movement through a general conference which we intended to convene in the near future. Dosa also emphasized the need for his government's help to enable the SLM to have its general conference.

The president listened attentively and responded in French. Dawsa volunteered to interpret. The president began by thanking us for the visit and for reaching the declaration of principles in Abuja. He stated that his government's foremost concern was the crisis in Darfur and how to bring about peace and allow all those affected people who lived in miserable conditions to go back home. He had done every thing possible within his means to resolve the issue amicably.

Chad's government and people had suffered from the crisis in Darfur and Darfur's security was inextricably linked to Chad's security. If there was no peace and security in Darfur, Chad also would be affected. The president said that although he had exerted every effort to reach a settlement between the government and the movements, his efforts were not appreciated. Instead, he had been accused by both parties of bias and support of the other party, but even so he was still willing to continue his efforts until there was peace in Darfur.

The president reminded us that in war both the victor and the vanquished were losers. On the issue of the movement's efforts to hold a general conference, he expressed his concerns about the divisions in the SLM. He emphasized that any division would weaken the overall movement and make it difficult to speak with one voice at the negotiating table, which in turn would make it difficult to achieve a comprehensive peace agreement, thus prolonging the crisis in Darfur. He expressed his willingness to help in terms of logistics and even the venue if the movement wished to hold the conference in Chad.

He concluded by asking what immediate plans we had on the issue of Shugar and Dr. Harir. I requested the president to facilitate their immediate return to N'Djamena and for us to hold talks with them to reach an amicable agreement. The president agreed and gave an immediate directive to send transportation to Bahai to convey them to N'Djamena. We felt relieved and delighted that the president agreed to help.

We expected the group to return within a few days in accordance to the president's directive, but they did not. Dawsa explained that there was no aircraft to be sent to Bahai, and traveling by land was difficult and hazardous due to the rainy season. Contacts were then made with Sultan Timan of Bahai to arrange the best way to convey them to N'Djamena.

Next we focused our attention on the issue of preparation for the general conference, which the Asmara meeting of February 2005 called for and reaffirmed in our acrimonious Tripoli meetings of July 2005.

We worked as team day and night. While Abdeljabar Dosa and Ali Trayo did all the difficult administrative tasks of working with computers and typing budgetary proposals, Adam Elnor, Mahjub Hissein, Harin, and myself did the remaining work of logistics, from putting out press statements on the date of the conference to phone calls to getting in contact with Dawsa's office for necessary support. We made Harin our liaison with Dawsa, for the two worked well together.

We laid emphasis on sending invitations first to the leadership, Abdulwahid Nor, Khamis Abakar and Minni Minnawi, then to creditable, tribally diversified members of the movement both within Darfur and abroad.

Dawsa took the initiative of contacting Abdulwahid and inviting him to Chad on behalf of the president and Chad mediation to judge for himself the preparations for the conference as well as Chad's neutrality on the issue of who would be the next chairman of the SLM. Harin assisted him. After several attempts they got him on phone in Asmara, but their conversation produced no favorable result as to Abdulwahid's visit to N'Djamena and participation in the preparatory work.

It was apparent that Dawsa was keenly favorable to Abdulwahid's reassertion through a general conference as the leader of the movement.

He had never favored Minni or anticipated his emergence as leader of the SLM. In fact, no one within the Chadian government ever favored Minni or any Zaghawa to be the head of the SLM. Both Abdulwahid, Khamis Abakar, Sharif Harir and even Suliman Jamos had their supporters within the Zaghawas in Déby's government. Why Minni lacked supporters with the Beri of Chad, it was not clear other than being viewed as an upstart,but why the Chad government did not want a Zaghawa to be the head of SLM, it was obvious that Idris Deby did not want to be perceived by Sudan government as helping his tribal person.

Regarding contact with Khamis, I took the initiative to contact him but the telephone network to Nairobi was so bad, I was not able to get through to him and resolved in the end to travel to him.

Our other efforts produced positive results. We received a large number of acceptances to our invitation proposals and confirmations for participation from eminent members of the movement such as Ibrahim Ahmed Ibrahim, Abakar Abulbashar, Mohammad Ibrahim Diba, Abdelhafiz Mustafa and others from the U.S., Europe and Saudi Arabia.

It was also during our stay in N'Djamena and work toward the success of the general conference that I, with some other SLM/SLA leaders, had the opportunity of meeting the U.S. Senator Joe Biden who was the chairman of U.S. Senate Committee on Foreign Affairs. He was on a fact-finding visit to the Darfur refugees in Eastern Chad. Our delegation was able to explain to the senator the situation on the ground and the progress of peace talks, or lack of it. Biden was so angered by the genocide and the condition of the refugees that he advocated in that meeting the importance of enforcing a no-fly zone over Darfur. Little did we know at the time that fate would play in favor of Biden to become the U.S. Vice President.

By end of October 2005, all necessary arrangements for the conference were completed and the international community and the media were informed, despite the beginning of the fourth round of peace talks in Abuja. However, some delegates from Europe were skeptical about the prospects of the conference being democratic. They left N'Djamena for Abuja and never returned to move with the rest of the delegates who entered Darfur for the conference.

CHAPTER TWENTY

𝒯he Haskanita Conference

Most leaders and commanders of SLM/SLA wanted the convening of the conference to put an end to the leadership tussle between Abdulwahid and Minni, as well as end the doubts on the position of Harir and others. As mentioned earlier it was also one of the provisions of a memoranda of understanding signed by the two in Asamara in February 2005 in the presence of more than twenty respected leaders of the movement.

While Abdelwahid never doubted his popularity among the internally displaced persons who by now their numbers reached two and half millions, and the refugees across the borders, Minni believed he was more popular with the SLA fighters, more especially he spent more time with them in the field and shared them their problems at a time Abdulwahid preferred to stay away in the comfort of Nairobi or Asmara. When the conference started there were high hopes that it would eventually produce legitimate leadership.

The arrival of the various delegates of the SLM/SLA and other supporters and guests to the town of Haskanita in November 2005 was not without a fanfare. There were chants of SLM slogans from the arriving delegates, welcoming shouts from the hosts and rapturous cries of exaltations from Haskanita women. Every household was ready to take any number of guests. Whole houses were vacated by their owners and offered as accommodation to the delegates and the various tribal cultural troupes. A large number of animals were slaughtered by Haskanita men and every family brought out the best of food it had reserved for such occasions. The women excelled in making the *Asida* porridge with *Tagalia* soup - Darfur's main dish. Traders of the market also offered whatever food items they were selling for free.

The conference officially commenced on November 3rd, 2005. It was preceded by a large and impressive cultural display from almost all Darfur tribal groups and a military parade by a contingent of SLA forces. The new SLA military band played well-known Sudanese martial music, which drew the attention of the foreign press, which came to cover the event, and observers alike. BBC correspondent John Fisher could not hide his admiration at the evolution of a militia force to a semi-regular force. So did Ron Cupps, the U.S. embassy observer of the conference, who counted every vehicle which took part in the parade. The parade and military salute were meant to honor the conference, dignitaries, and the chief hosts Abdulwahid – in case he attended - Minni Minnawi, Joma Haqar and Ustaz Ibrahim Ahmed Ibrahim the conference chairman.

In his opening remarks, the chairman of the conference Ustaz Ibrahim Ahmed Ibrahim pledged to run truly transparent democratic elections and made a special appeal to the chairman of the movement, Abdulwahid Mohammad Nur, to attend the conference.

Both the opening and later proceedings were also attended by representatives from the international community, namely the United Nations, the African Union peacekeeping mission in Darfur, and the governments of United States and Libya, though the later withdrew from the proceedings at a later stage. But it was the U.S. Embassy in Khartoum's representative, Mr. Ron Cupps, and the UN point person, Mariana Nolte, who had the most presence in the proceedings. I personally with Ustaz Trayo Ali took the responsibility of simultaneous/consecutive English interpreting of all the proceedings to the American and UN representatives.

Minni Minnawi wanted the chairmanship of the movement and he had tirelessly worked for it. I believe he had every right to aspire to any position within the movement and gain it through the democratic and legitimate means. There were those of us who wanted Minni to be the chairman, but only through genuine democratic means. There was also others even within the perceived Minni group who wanted Abdulwahid to reassert and be confirmed as chairman. I believe there was nothing politically wrong with that. It only showed the democratic nature of the movement.

Abdulwahid's Absence and the ascending of Minni

From the onset it was very clear that the whole event was dominated by the SLA rather than the SLM,or the representatives of the IDPs and refugees, and by the personality of Juddo Isa (Saqor). He was the real king maker, more especially since the SLA took the lion's share in terms of numbers of voting delegates. Out of eight hundred voting delegates, more than four hundred were SLA who were loyal to Jodo and by extension, to Minni.

It was an anomalous situation where in any case Abdulwahid could not have turned the tide against Minni easily, given the loyalty of the majority of SLA personnel in Haskanita to Minni. Had it been that the two sections of the SLM and SLA in Jebel Marra and below the Jebel jointly sent their delegates to the organizing committee headed by both Ibrahim Ahmed Ibrahim, a Birgid, and Alrayah Mahmoud, a Massalit - two men whose integrity could not be questioned - and had it been that Abdulwahid campaigned heavy among the delegates in Haskanita, there might have been a different outcome. Only then could Abdulwahid have challenge Minni, given the fact that a sizeable number of the civilian delegates, even within the Zaghawas, were in support of Abdulwahid.

Abdulwahid rejected all efforts to bring him and his loyalists to the conference any where within Darfur. There was a time a suggestion was made that he could propose the venue which suited him provided it was within SLA/SLM controlled areas in Darfur, but he was against the idea. He wanted to hold the conference in Libya, an idea which was rejected by the commanders on the ground. With his absence, he lost a golden opportunity to be the undisputed leader of the movement.

It was his realization of this fact which made him send a last minute five member delegation headed by Ahmed Abdelshafi and Nesraldin to make an effort at postponing the event. The request came too late and was justifiably refused by the committee which helped organize the conference and spent a lot of time at trying to convince Abdulwahid to come to the conference.

It is also worth mentioning that some key figures also boycotted the conference, leaders such as Dr. Sharif Harir, Adam Shugar, and most well known members from the Massalit and Fur tribes, especially those based overseas.

The proceeding of the conference ran smoothly and everything was done according to the rules of the game of democracy. Mr. Cupps the American commented on the way the conference was conducted by saying it was "participatory, democratic and transparent".

There were three contestants to the position of chairmanship: Minni Minnawi, Adam Bakhit, and Suliman Jamos, but the later withdrew just before the ballot. Minni won the vote by a wide margin. A vote was also taken for the post of vice chairman and secretary general. They were won by Dr. Alrayah Mahmoud from the Massalit tribe and Nustafa Tirab from the Fur tribe. A revolutionary command council was also selected,to be headed by Isa Bahreldin from Berti tribe.

At one stage, some SLA commanders became disaffected at the prospect of Minni emerging as the new chair of the movement, so they boycotted the conference at the voting stage. These included Bakhit Karima, the deputy commander general of the SLA, Arko Suliman Dahya and others.

Dissension in the Ranks

Bakhit Karima and Arko Suliman Dahya were two very influential and highly respected commanders within the SLA. They belong to the first generation of officers who founded the SLA along with Minni and Abdalla Abakar. Karima was operations commander,he first became the Deputy Commander General of the SLA after the death of Abdalla Abaker and elevation of Juma Haqar to Commander General, while Dahya – a younger brother to Omar Dahya - was a sectoral commander before being wounded in mid-2003.

At the time of Haskanita conference, the two were still loyal to the ideals of the SLA/SLM and to the original structure of the movement with Minni as the Secretary General and Abdulwahid as Chairman. While it is hard to speculate that Bakhit Karima nursed greater ambition and a greater role within the SLA, because of his limited education and training, it was explicit that Arko Dahya, a university graduate, was not content with both his own position and Minni's leadership ambition in the SLA/SLM.

Minni was aware of this fact and often dealt with him with caution and diligence, sometimes placating and sometimes cajoling him into neutralization on major policy decisions. At the stalemate during the negotiations on fourth round, both were sent to Abuja with other commanders by the SLA high command to help break the deadlock. Though their arrival did not produce any agreement, it helped reduce Abdulwahid's intransigence within the Abuja group, as some of these were the very people already in the field when the SLA came into being in late 2002.

At the voting stage of the conference both Bakhit and Arko were absent. It was rumored that they were against the process being conducted and they might stage an action which might stop it, even if it meant violence and death. Minni's body guards beefed up security around him.

The absence of Bakhit and Arko from the voting stages of the conference worried many delegates and put a question mark to the loyality of those fighters under them to Minni, more especially as the two left Haskanita with a sizeable number of fighters without informing the commander general Goma Haqar or Minni. Meanwhile other commanders with forces in Haskanita, such as Jodo Shagor,Mohamadein Orgajor,Ahmed Abudegin, Nuradin Elyas and others remained loyal to Minni and the outcome of the process.

After the election, Minni was advised to spend greater time reaching out to Bakhiet and Arko to regain their support or at least neutralize them. That was the main reason made Minni to skip the the Nairobi meeting with the US deputy secretary of state Mr R. Zolleck.

US Concern and the Nairobi Conference, November 2005

The absence of Abdulwahid from the conference and emergence of Minni as the new elected leader of the movement worried Washington, despite the excellent report written by Ron Cupps on the proceedings of the conference. Washington clearly discerned the division of the movement into two factions, the Haskanita faction and the Jebel Marra faction, where Abdulwahid remained.

The morning after the elections, we received word from Mr. Cupps that the deputy secretary of state, Mr. Robert Zolleck, wanted to meet with fifteen top leaders from both the SLM and SLA in Nairobi, Kenya to discuss the peace process and the way forward. There was a sense of urgency in the way Mr. Cupps delivered Mr. Zolleck's message.

An emergency meeting was held in the new residence of the new deputy chairman of the movement, Alrayah Mahmoud, to study the American request. There was a mood of excitement as we felt American recognition to the outcome of the conference and possible support. In attendance was a select group of political leaders from the SLM as well as SLA commanders. Though I insisted on staying away from the meeting to give the new deputy chairman the chance to exercise his own judgment with the help of others elected to various positions of the new structure, I was requested to attend.

The meeting briefly discussed the possible scenarios which the delegation might face in Nairobi, but we never imagined that Abdulwahid and his group would be in attendance. The meeting went into a selection process and again I insisted that I would like to be excluded from the delegation to Nairobi, but again there was insistence from the both the deputy chairman and the rest of the meeting. Minni, too, lent his voice on the issue. It was also agreed that Minni should remain behind to reach out to the dissenting commanders. Two days after the conference our delegation which headed by the new deputy chairman Dr Alrayah Mahmoud left Haskanita on African Union Helikopters to Alfashir. At the air port we met UN personell and a UN plane that would transport us to Kenya.

The UN chartered transport plane took off from Alfashir Airport on the afternoon of November 17th, 2005 and flew directly to Nairobi international airport. It was a little after dusk when we landed at Jomo Kenyata International airport. We were check in through a special immigration counter, and transported to a hotel in the city.

Until the next day, we were not aware of the agenda of the meeting with Mr. Zolleck or who would be in attendance. At about seven in the morning I came out of my room and walked toward the lobby of the hotel for my morning tea, where to my surprise I met some SLM/A members who were known Abdulwahid loyalists. I exchanged greetings with them and hurried back to the rooms of some of my group to alert them of the possibility of meeting Abdulwahid and his group.

The following hours we were conveyed to the venue of the meeting, only to find Abdulwahid and his group already seated there. Our delegation decided to walk out, insisting that it would not recognize Abdulwahid, as now there is a new leadership produced by the Haskanita conference that was recognized by the U.S. government but boycotted by Abdulwahid.

The U.S. delegation accompanying Mr. Zolleck included Ms. Jendayi Frazer, the then Assistant Secretary of State for African Affairs; Ambassador Charles Snyder; Ambassador Yates, Mr. Roger Winter, the US charge de affaires in Sudan, and others. They made frantic efforts to get us back in to the room to sit us together but we refused. Eventually the U.S. delegation met with each delegation separately. At the end of the meetings, a joint communiqué was prepared by the U.S. delegation of Mr. Zolleck, which reiterated among other things that the SLM should remain one and work together to achieve peace in the region. Our delegation refused to sign the statement.

Mr. Zolleck became furious and demanded an immediate meeting with the leader of our delegation, Dr. Alrayah Mahmoud. I went with Alrayah to the meeting to act as an interpreter. Zolleck expressed his disappointment in our position and the fact that Minni Minnawi declined to come to Nairobi to meet him. Both Alrayah and I apologized and explained the circumstances which forced Minnawi to stay away from meeting him. Whether Mr. Zolleck accepted our explanation or not, we could not tell, as he ended the meeting without further comment.

CHAPTER TWENTY ONE

Fifth Round of Talks and the DPA

When the fifth round of talks began in late December 2005, the SLM/SLA had already become two different factional movements with two separate organizational hierarchies and two separate delegations to the peace talks. The efforts of the American government the previous November to keep the movement united had no or little success.

Each of the two factions sent to the talks a large delegation, comprised mainly of expatriate members based in Europe or the Gulf states, while the actual commanders in the field had little representation. The hope of the international community was that the movements at least adopt unified positions at the negotiating table with the Sudan government. Working out the joint position was a surprisingly an easy task. Both the JEM and Abdulwahid's group showed readiness to work with the Haskanita faction.

The movements also adopted an internal code of conduct regarding the negotiations with the government, which was in effect the maintenance of secrecy on negotiating positions before going to meetings with the government side and mediation.

For the first time, both Khalil Ibrahim and Abdulwahid Nur were present at the talks. Minni was on and off. He roved between Asmara and Tripoli. The head of the negotiating team on the SLM Haskanita side was Abdeljabar Dosa, who acted in previous rounds of talks as chief negotiator when Dr. Harir declined to appear.

The format of the negotiations was dictated by the African Union and it was along the tradition of the Naivasha format, which was on three commissions - the power sharing commission, the wealth sharing commission, and the security arrangements commission. The attempt by the movements to add a joint assessment commission was rebuffed by the mediation.

On strategy and tactics of negotiation, the movements were not found lacking. Some of Darfur's most enlightened and informed personalities were brought in as advisors to help the movements draft their position paper. Both Professor Sidiq Ambada and Dr. Mosa Karama played vital roles in conceptualizing and drafting the wealth sharing document. The renouned Darfur historian and expert, the Norwaigian Rex O'Fahey was also invited for expert openion on tribal lands or Hawakir matters.

About two months in to the talks, Minni returned to the venue. Not quite a week from his return, he had the bad news from Darfur that his father died, while a day or two later his sister also died in a tragic car accident while traveling to attend her father's funeral. The two incidents bore heavily on him and made him rather detached from the goings on at the venue of the talks, but he was quick to recover and follow the talks.

The Deaths of Juddo Shaqor and Nuradin Elias

Around the beginning of March 2006, the talks between our group and the government reach a near collapse. It was also rumored that Abdulwahid's group was closer to a peace agreement than any other group. It seemed two people were beginning to play key roles at persuading Abdulwahid. One was a government minister and Abdulwahid's own kinfolk, Mohammad Yusif, and Sudan expert Alex de Waal.

The details to which these two went to persuade the Abdulwahid group was not clear to us; but it was clear that despite the adopted code of conduct on dealing with the government side - which our own faction adhered to in spirit and letter - both Abdulwahid and his chief negotiators broke the rules. They were seen on occasions in public eye of Chida Hotel freely exchanging compliments and holding discussions with the members of the government delegation.

There was a time the venue was flooded with almost every notable personality in Darfur: traditional tribal chiefs, professionals, former government functionaries, and even Janjaweed leaders. One of these was the notorious Adam Police, a one-time suspected bank robber in Neyala town, who was seen having a discussion with Abdulwahid in an exclusive Abuja restaurant away from the Chida hotel.

These rumors made us fear that the already divided front would be more fractured if the SLM headed by Abdulwahid signed a unilateral deal with the government, with huge losses to the people of Darfur. Nobody knew what Minni was thinking when he held few meetings with the delegation on his own, but not even in our wildest imaginings did we think he could contemplate a preemptive deal with the government.

The head of our negotiating team, Abdeljabar Dosa, was a sincere man, motivated to achieve good results for the movements and for the people of Darfur. He put his cousin Ali Dosa in charge of the coordination of negotiating files. Ibrahim Ahmed Ibrahim, formerly a Umma party loyalist and the man who competently ran the Haskanita conference, was placed in charge of the power sharing commission. Lastly, Eltijani Albador, an old friend of his and also Umma loyalist, was put in charge of wealth sharing. Albador was a recluse, elderly gentleman with dynamism to the meager, who enjoyed the prestige and trappings attached to the title of Wealth Sharing Commission Chairman rather than the actual burdens and responsibilities demanded by it.

Toward the end of the third month into the talks, the government offensives against the positions of the SLA/SLM in Darfur increased. There were reports almost on a daily basis about serious clashes between government forces sypported by Janjaweed and the SLA in Central and Eastern Darfur. Hundreds of thousands of African civilians were displaced as a result of arial bombardment and fighting,and their villages burned. In one of these clashes some of the finest SLA commanders were targeted and killed by snipers shots. Judo Isa (Shaqor), the *de facto* commander of the SLA, was also killed along with Noradin Ilyas, a sectoral commander.

The death of the two commanders Jodo and Noradin dealt a serious blow to the SLA, Haskanita military and to Minni personally. It was more of blow than even the loss of Abdalla Abakar because Jodo combined both Abdalla's physical courage and his own personal military initative. Jodo was a gallant soldier with fighting prowess not surpassed by any fighter.

Minni grieved their deaths as did every one in our group, but Minni's grief which had major consequences on his morale and the spirit with which we pursued the talks at Abuja. At one point I felt Minni almost lost faith in the struggle against a government so entrenched and so formidable. He felt like a general who lost every soldier in the battle field.

Pressure in the Hour of Grief Produces the DPA

By April 2005, there were lots of rumors regarding the SLM/ Abdulwahid faction's dealings with the government delegation. Members of government delegation were seen routinely going in and out of the hotel rooms of prominent members of the SLM/Abdulwahid faction,such as Dr Abdelrahman Musa his chief negotiator and Ibrahim Madipo his power sharing commission head, and it was rumored that his faction would soon sign an agreement with the government.

Abdulwahid seemed evasive and non-committal on any specific position, but from all indications he seemed to have dreamed of an agreement which would make him the nominee to the highest position proposed in the agreement, and would in all respect loved to snatch it if things were cast on a level field. His chief negotiators were much more eager and ready to be the spoilers had he bluffed or rejected.

In the SLM/Haskanita camp, there were attempts by the Libyan government to arrange a separate track of talks with government. Minni was invited on several occasions to go to Tripoli to meet with top government representatives. I voiced my objection to a separate track which would leave out the negotiating team in Abuja.

At one point, the Sudan Vice President Ali Authman Taha held direct talks with Minni accompanied by Abdel Aziz Sam the legal advisor of the delegation, but the official position of our delegation in Abuja was that there would not be any concession on the demands we earlier laid out with the other movements.

By end of April, the AU mediation suffered from fatigue and dwindling resources, and so proposed a deadline of a week whereby either the parties reach an agreement or declare the failure of the talks.

The deadline arrived without a clear breakthrough, and we prepared for the AU mediation's declaration of the end of the talks without an agreement. Everyone in the international community became worried, especially the U.S. delegation which had invested so much in the Darfur crisis and the success of the peace talks.

Then a request came from the U.S. delegation for deference of the declaration for three days, within which efforts would be made to bring the parties closer to an agreement. The mediation accepted the request.

During the three days which followed, intense pressure was placed on the leaders of the movements, Abdulwahid, Minni and Khalil. The pressure came from top dignitaries such as President Obasanjo of Nigeria, President Denis Sassou-Ngueso of Congo Brazaville, and Mr. Zolleck, the Deputy Secretary of State for the U.S.

Both Abdulwahid and Khalil were able to withstand the pressure and refused to sign the agreement. However, Minni, who was already weakened by the grief of the death of his loved ones and losses of men like Judo Shaqor and Noradin Ilyas, was ready to give it a try, although he knew that to Khartoum, the agreement was just a piece of paper and would do everything possible not to implement it. Minni also counted on the Americans to support him, but the events later showed that the U.S. was not ready to give him the full support he needed to counter the Khartoum sharks.

Falling Apart

After Minni signed the agreement, there was resentment and outright objections from the SLM/SLA delegation. Well- respected leaders such commander Salah Abderahim "Jook" and Ibrahim Ahmed Ibrahim were on the verge of issuing press statements declaring rejection of the agreement and defection from the SLM/Haskanita.

Despite my disagreement with Minni's signing of the agreement, I acted as a pacifier between the the objectors and acceptors of the peace deal to avert a breakup of the movement right there in Abuja. I invited both Salah Jook and Ibrahim Ahmed Ibrahim separately in to my hotel room and talked them in to accepting the decision of Minni for now, and work toward the unity of our movement until such a time that we will be able to face the government united and they accepted.

Following May 5th, the night of the agreement, the whole party of the movements fell into disarray. Many left Abuja vowing to carry on with the resistance, since then Darfur did not see the peace it needed. On the ground the government intensified its attacks through out Darfur on civilian targets it believed to be sanctuaries of hold out rebels. The death toll among the African population of Fur, Massalit,Zaghawa and others as a result of attacks and hunger and desease exceeded three hundred thousands by UN estimates. It was an ethnic cleansing and genocide per excellence.

Minni himself with few advisors who persuaded him to accept the deal left for Darfur to lay the ground work for the new reality.

EPILOGUE

The Future of Darfur

The future of Darfur was not reflected upon and subjected to serious scrutiny and consideration by the sons and daughters of Darfur, whether at the time the British were ruling the region as part of the Anglo-Egyptian Sudan or during their exit from Sudan, or in the years which followed Sudan's independence.

Despite the crude and harsh treatment by those who gained the control of the reins of power at the exit of the British from Sudan, Darfuris were acquiescent with the policies of Khartoum on their affairs. Khartoum played on the complexities and differences of the Darfuri society and continued to rule the region in the British style, sending administrators and security chiefs from their Jallaba sons.

They formed, as the British did, a class of their own, completely detaching themselves from the people of the communities they were posted to rule. Until the 1980s, no Darfuri occupied a position of governor of a province, even in Darfur.

Darfur was kept, as in the Colonial Era, in a state of perpetual backwardness and ignorance. It was regarded, despite its huge potentials, agricultural and other resources and contributions to the Sudanese economy, as - to use Professor Gerard Prunie's words, a remote out post; an appendage to a larger ensemble and in no position to influence any Sudanese policy.

But unlike the British administrators who had no need for the so-regarded at the time, meager resources of Darfur and Darfuris, the

Jallaba semi-Colonial administrators who came from poorer region of the Northern province were greedy. They came to Darfur to consume and exploit both the resources and the people. This shows why for so long Darfuris were kept undereducated and untrained in leadership roles, as Dr. Sharif Harir states in his book, *Short-Cut to Decay,* which chronicles the injustice done by ruling elites to the marginalized areas and people.

Darfuris and Darfur itself will be better off without any centralized authority which ties them somewhere outside Darfur itself, where they remain a marginalized minority in the affairs of the country, third-class citizens who have little or no control even on Darfur affairs.

Experience has shown, both in past and recent history, that Darfuris benefit from Darfur itself and not from the Nilotic Sudan. When the economic opportunity of working outside of Darfur was offered, they benefited from countries like Libya, Saudi Arabia and the neighboring countries on the west and West Africa.

Khartoum benefits from Darfur, politically and economically, more than Darfur has ever benefited from Khartoum. Culturally and socially the Jalaba establishment controlled every sphere and walk of life at the center. As the southerners before,the policies of the establishment made it impossible for Darfuris and the rest of the marginalized groups to integrate and blend with each other to produce homogniety in terms of culture and race. When Darfuris needed the help of the rest of Sudanese society in the time of genocide by their own government, that society was acquiescent with the regime's policies or at least silent to what was going on in Darfur. Khartoum society and Northerners in general identified themselves or tuned into events in Middle East, Gaza and Egypt in particular, rather than Darfur.

At a time when human rights groups from around the world felt the Darfuri pain and pressured their governments to do some thing about Darfur, Khartoumers demonstrated in support of Hamas or Hezbollah.

Any attempt by a group with a large number of Darfuris to gain political power is viewed by the riverine Sudanese as a racist attempt; there after, Darfuris in general are targeted and persecuted.

This disregard and acquiescence with the regime at the height of the genocide leaves the Darfur people with the feeling that the rest of the country doesn't feel or even understand their plight, or if it notices it, the country doesn't care. The Darfur people are left to fend for themselves with the international community.

The present crisis will linger for some time, with greater suffering of the Darfuris in the refugee and IDP camps unless the Darfur sons and daughters bury their differences and tribal affiliation prejudices and focus on the causes and the objectives of the struggle.

Darfuris, whether Africans or Arabs, are people highly assimilated and integrated to the extent that you can hardly find a family which is not intermarried with the other ethnic groups. All Darfur Arabs have blood relations with Zaghawa, Fur, Massalit and others; likewise, the Fur, Massalit, Zaghawa and others have blood relations with the different Darfur Arabs.

The Darfur people must unite if they want to end the present crisis and achieve freedom for their country.

Darfur can stand on its own; it has the resources, both mineral and agricultural. It has the human capital, while the international community will help in the technical know-how of utilizing these resources. Its neighboring countries such as Libya and Chad were never better off than Darfur in the past, but because of the freedom they had, they were able to develop their resources and today are in a better position than Darfur.

There is always a room for the Khartoum government to maneuver and be in control if Darfuris allow their tribal differences to dominate their relations. We must instead unite for the sake of Darfur. In the light of the absence of attractive unity with the rest of Sudan, we are better off alone.

If the international community is keen on helping Sudan and Darfur resolve the present crisis, it should help Darfuris realize their self-determination.

Great achievements in history began with dreams, conceptualization and articulation of those dreams, and then putting them into effect. Darfuris must dream of their own state, their own constitution, their own national identity. They must dream of their own art, culture, theatres, opera houses and museums. They must dream of their own international airports, highways, bridges, metroline and subways in Alfashir, Neyala, Genina,Kutum and other cities. All these are possible and attainable if we bury our differences and focus on how to win the cause.

Remaining under Khartoum in the present circumstances will only perpetuate our second class status in the national scheme of issues. The Jallaba elite will never accept equality with Darfuris or anyone from the marginalized areas. For them, Sudan is theirs and anyone else from Kurdufan, Darfur, the East, and the South Blue Nile must remain second or third class citizens.

This state of affairs will continue unless the marginalized unite and effect change at the center. In the absence of this unity, Darfur should seek to affect one and build their own nation.

www.ingramcontent.com/pod-product-compliance
Lightning Source LLC
Chambersburg PA
CBHW030441290526
45786CB00001B/397